Praise

'Ramita's experiences as both a mom and a mentor to countless girls and their parents have set her apart as an empathetic leader who shows us not that girls need to change, but that we, as caring and capable adults, can and should change the world to better support them. Her compassionate approach will inspire parents, teachers, and coaches to think critically about the world of girls and how mentoring girls can make their and our lives richer.'
— **Michelle Icard**, author of *Fourteen Talks by Age Fourteen*

'Anyone living or working with teenagers should read this book, a practical and well-researched guide that is not only fit for our times but also written from personal experience. It's a must-read in service of setting up the next generation.'
— **Andrew Sheridan**, Master Certified Coach

GIRL ELEVATED

Five steps to empower girls in early adolescence to be their best

RAMITA ANAND

Rᵉthink

First published in Great Britain in 2022
by Rethink Press (www.rethinkpress.com)

Illustrations by Chloe Chang

For my mama, whose light shines brightest among the stars and guides me every day.

This book is dedicated to my children, Siena and Ishaan, my raison d'être; my husband, Paras, whose never-ending love has encouraged me to be my best every day; and my siblings, who lift and champion me at every stage of life. Lastly, but most crucially, of course, this is for all the super-girls out there making the world a better place.

Contents

Introduction

Raising girls who are in early adolescence involves excitement and angst in equal measure. Their new-found independence and their desire to express their unique identities are crucial at this stage. The worry and confusion parents experience at what is unfolding, though, can result in despair and/or a desire to keep their precious girls little and protected for as long as possible. It's our role to prepare girls for the life that awaits them, but our help can feel unwelcome when they think that they already know everything.

As a teen, I struggled with loss and change. I became a teacher specialising in middle and primary school education in diverse schools, and then trained to work in schools with children who have additional needs. I'm also the mother of a neurodiverse child. I draw on my story to support parents, educators and other professionals working with girls in early adolescence. My experience teaching in schools internationally for over fifteen years has taught me valuable lessons about the multitude of changes young girls face in their middle school years. My goal is to help develop strategies to lift and empower girls to be the best possible versions of themselves.

This led me to create and develop an educational mentoring service, Elevate.RA, which supports girls in early adolescence to unleash their inner powers and be passionate learners. Based on the thoughtfully designed lesson plans, case studies and real-life, practical methods devised for Elevate.RA, this book will assist parents raising girls and support the educators who influence girls' lives daily through the most challenging parts of teen-girl development.

My interest in supporting children with additional challenges came after my son, now eleven years old, was diagnosed with autism at four years old. Working through his development cognitively, socially, emotionally and physically has taught me so much about neurodiversity. It's crucial for us parents and educators to champion every child, no matter their make-up. We must encourage them to pursue their dreams while keeping their confidence up. Because of this conviction, my personal experience as a mother, and subsequent professional research and development of new methods, my mission to support children with learning, social and emotional challenges has become a passion.

The experiences I had in my tween and adolescent years were instrumental in shaping the adult I've become. When I was thirteen, I lost my mother to cancer. This was undoubtedly the darkest period of my life. My teenage years were spent without my mother, who'd been my role model, best friend and teacher. I was also charged with the care of my two younger siblings while my father worked, which wasn't always an easy task, to say the least. I strongly believe that it was the confidence and self-belief instilled by my mother that helped me pursue my own passion for education.

I understand the tricky teen years, and how it feels to be the odd one out. I was often the only girl who didn't have her mother at matches or recitals, and that loneliness is still all too familiar to me. I have a great deal of empathy for young girls who face challenges and have to grow up on a path that might look different to their peers'. No girl should feel alone on this journey. My goal is to provide girls and their parents with allyship and lift them up so they move upwards and onwards. My journey towards growth has taught me to persevere. I've also learned how to use education, honesty and exploration to keep myself grounded, full of the strength and optimism necessary to face each day with renewed courage. It's my hope that my personal experiences and stories of evolution and discovery will help girls recognise their potential and inherent self-worth.

Many parents are worried that their daughters won't fulfil their potential. We, as parents, tend to harbour shame, fear and blame around our daughters' progress and development, especially if they don't meet expectations set by others. It's also common to be bombarded with feelings of defeat and confusion when trying to understand our daughters and their emerging and developing complexities. Every girl has a unique learning style and also an individual personality which, combined with the physical and emotional changes of adolescence, can feel overwhelming.

It's only natural that we, as parents who have limited time, energy and means, can become frustrated with our girls and/or the seemingly never-ending cycle of emotional ups and downs. I understand and relate to this wholeheartedly.

This is why I want to impress upon you the value of preventative education. As a society, we have embraced preventative medicine. Similarly, our girls can benefit from being taught strategies that will help them face the changes of their middle school years with greater confidence and poise. I like to call these strategies and tools 'superpowers'.

My five-step methodology brings together the five superpowers that I focus on in the work I do and explore here in depth:

1. Confidence

2. Empathy

3. Emotional intelligence

4. Resilience

5. Kindness

There's a growing body of research and evidence that describes the dangers a young girl can face if she doesn't actively learn about these five superpowers in her most impressionable time of growth.[1] Setting up young girls with strong armour and a foundation on which their next phase of development can be built will prepare them for the unpredictable roller coaster of adult life. My experience has shown me that creating opportunities for girls who are between the vulnerable ages of nine and thirteen to be counselled and guided by a dedicated educational mentor can lead to remarkable breakthroughs.

Enabling our girls to understand, develop and harness their superpowers will equip them for the inevitable curveballs growing up involves. If we can teach them to lean in, accept themselves and unlearn some of the social conditioning that has been fed to them, we all, as a society, will reap the benefits and move forward in the right direction.

Parenting and educating early adolescents takes us into a new role. With younger children, we tend to provide all the solutions. We know which snack will make life better again. With early adolescents, who are facing evolving friendships, test-result pressures and fashion faux pas, our position as parents and teachers becomes more subtle. It's now time to be the supporting coach who provides girls enough freedom to make their own judgement calls secure in the knowledge that they can reach into their toolbelt of strategies, and who's also there with a snack and a hug when needed. While parents play a crucial role in raising their daughters, at this time of development, girls are trying to form their identities away from their parents. Therefore, the roles of other adults in their lives, namely teachers and coaches, become even more relevant. The valuable input educators can have at this time in a girl's life is not to be undermined, which is why I've written this book through the lens of a parent while offering ideas and strategies for educators also.

Girl Elevated includes real-life case studies of girls' authentic experience and well-researched ideas - with the use of 'girl' and 'woman' throughout referring to anyone who identifies as a girl or woman. I've combined some of the most insightful takeaways from thought leaders, researchers, seekers, activists and creatives whose work has fed into the Elevate.RA mission. These findings and the experience from my practice enable me to deliver a unique, refreshing and proven method to help you help your girls be their best selves, adopt a learner's mindset of curiosity and passion, and reach for the stars.

My vision for the future is to be part of a society where all differences are celebrated. Where girls aren't seen as inferior. Where girls can learn to be smart, confident women who lead with compassion and kindness and exemplify courage and strength. The best way to achieve this goal is to work with young girls at the most impactful stages of their growth. All my lessons incorporate my ethos: that each and every girl is an actual, real-life superhero. She may be in training, but all heroes require help from time to time to achieve their goals.

Raising girls isn't always easy, but you needn't be alone. As they say, it takes a village, and together we're stronger. Are you ready to discover ways to lift our girls so they can unleash their power? Let's dive in.

ONE

Setting The Scene: Why Elevate?

Before taking off

When girls rise, we rise.

There is overwhelming evidence available today that corroborates what many educators and parents have known for years: in too many areas, girls are unable to reach their full potential.

More often than not, the root of the problem involves our collective attitudes and beliefs about girls. These affect adolescent girls' self-esteem and can have real consequences on their educational progress. Girls need us to be their champions. The effects of elevating girls, which include decreased poverty, economic growth and stronger families, can be felt globally.[2]

Providing girls with opportunities for growth and education is the essence of creating a better world for all. This chapter will explore some key areas that can impact and limit a girl's full potential and how parents and educators can work to remove these barriers.

At the forefront of any parent and carer's mind is ensuring they raise their girls to be the happiest they possibly can be. Many of the experiences we have as a teen shape the adults we become and the confidence with which we lead our lives or view the world. Therefore, establishing a strong foundation from which to develop a strong self-belief is key.

The KWP (knowledge, wonder, power) framework

When faced with hard truths about their girls struggling in any area of growth, such as school or friendships, some parents may choose to ignore them or assume that everything will work out on its own. Others may spiral into fear and panic. Many parents blame their daughters and believe that laziness, lack of diligence or poor motivation is the cause of the challenges they're facing.

No one wants to hear that their daughter is having learning difficulties, and many people have a hard time accepting it. Our knee-jerk reaction may be to schedule extra tuition time, sign them up for booster lessons or find the nearest enrichment centre. In cases where a lack of diligence and motivation is the reality, these programmes can add value – if the concerns are based solely on academic achievements. They aren't necessarily right for everyone, though, and they don't take into account the many complexities that can cause our daughters to find themselves slipping. Even the most confident girls can feel uncertain during this period of change, as both their bodies and brains develop. Changes in hormones and the limbic system impact everything from self-control to decision-making,[3] leading to changes that may surprise both the parents and the girls.

It's often not a matter of 'not trying hard enough'. There can be, and commonly are, greater invisible barriers to their success in the middle years.

The KWP principles developed and designed within the Elevate.RA mentoring service provide a constructive framework to lift young girls who are vulnerable at this crucial stage of development to become the best versions of themselves. These overarching principles underpin the Elevate.RA journey. They can be beneficial academically but also offer a skillset that can be built upon throughout the rest of a girl's life. If their girls are shown how to adopt this framework, parents can be confident in their daughters' future, knowing that the key attributes they need to navigate the ups and downs of life have been firmly embedded.

Knowledge

Within the KWP framework, *K* stands for *knowledge*. The aim is to begin the journey by bringing awareness to the fact that our girls already have amazing abilities and attributes. It's essential for them to recognise how many fabulous traits they already possess. Unsurprisingly, given the staggering statistics regarding low self-esteem in teen and tween (generally judged as about 9–14 years old) girls today,[4] they often find this process challenging. They require reassurance.

I've seen many girls who are shocked to realise that, after some encouragement, they can come up with a lengthy list that elucidates their creativity in art, their talents in baking, the kindness they show their friends, the support they offer at home with siblings, or their achievements on the netball court, for example. As this list takes shape, their eyes widen with each reminder that they already have powers within them that are worth celebrating. Starting our work from a place of positivity and celebration ensures that girls are less sceptical of my intentions and lets them know that I won't be lecturing them – instead, our journey will be focused on my working *with* them, so that they can be their own champions.

Wonder

The next phase of the framework is *W*, which stands for *wonder*, or *worries*, which we all have when we let our girls out into the world on their own. Sadly, the world, especially of late, has been full of negativity. Everything from the news to conversations overheard at the bus stop plays a part in shaping the worries that creep into the minds of young girls. During our work together, this phase is a great opportunity for parents, teachers and girls to explore the worries that they're experiencing together. Often, just voicing concerns without expecting solutions makes the weight of carrying these burdens so much lighter. Writing them out also frees up space in the mind, decreasing the weight our girls carry every day. There's so much to digest in the world. Compound that with the physical and mental changes they're facing, and it shouldn't surprise you that giving our girls an opportunity to be heard can alleviate a huge amount of the tension that has undoubtedly built up.

Many of the common worries expressed do originate from deep-rooted pressures around academic achievement. Parents can believe that the only way to rectify the situation is to sign up their daughter for more lessons and extra study time. This approach fails to address the root of the problem. Extra lessons won't help girls overcome the obstacles necessary to be ready to learn. We must examine the foundational issues that prevent our daughters from being their best selves. Many barriers exist today, and few occur in isolation. Here are some to consider:

- Underlying learning difficulties, such as dyslexia or dyspraxia; issues with concentration, attention, focus, working memory, anxiety or sensory overload; or auditory processing concerns

- Grief or loss of family members

- A family move

- Parental pressure

- Parental absence (when long work hours or travel keep parents away from their children)

- Friendship and / or bullying concerns, which can be amplified by social media

- Economic pressures (children pick up on our unconscious attitudes and may compare themselves to their more advantaged peers)

- Fatigue

- Diet (access to and awareness of healthy foods is key)

- Mental health concerns (not feeling good enough or having low self-worth)

Many professionals can help with the barriers mentioned above. As the parent of a child with learning challenges, I've consulted many specialists. Employing their expertise is crucial. These barriers need to be fully understood before we can even begin to evaluate their effects on our daughters' well-being, though. This stage of the framework engages both parents and their daughters to dissect some of these important roadblocks which can be an understandable source of worry.

Power

Finally, *P* is about recognising how we create *power* from the challenges we face. It's about helping our girls unleash their inner power! After going through this framework, girls will be stronger, more compassionate, and self-assured. They will have developed a skillset that will provide them with methods to cope in times of adversity; they'll be more comfortable facing challenges in their new armour of superpowers. Not only will this benefit them in their daily family life and school experiences – it will also make them better citizens. Girls who equip themselves with empathy, resilience, confidence, emotional literacy and kindness will shatter those glass ceilings and shape our future for the better.

Ultimately, adopting the five superpowers and using the KWP framework as guidance will support girls to see the world as a beautiful mix of colours and people with unique styles – including unique learning styles.

The five-step methodology around how we can give our girls the best foundation follows in the chapters ahead. Some of the key ingredients for us to take a closer look at before implementing those superpowers include three overarching factors that can impact our girls' abilities to be content, and confident in themselves. In the first instance, we must look at the way in which we currently measure happiness and success, then examine how the introduction of social media applications has impacted girls and their mental health in recent years and, thirdly, it is key to understand the value in role models who represent the girls in a more genuine and authentic way – not in an overly curated, unattainable depiction of girls and women who may only represent one part of our society. Representation across all disciplines, whether it be politics, fashion, film or finance and technology, is crucial. Our girls will only find ways to feel like they can also achieve their dreams and reach new heights if they see such role models in their social media feeds, for example. Girls can learn to accept themselves better if they look up to other successful women who are relatable to them, thus feeling happier in who they are from within and diminishing the need to seek external validation or compare themselves to unrealistic beauty standards.

Girls and social media

As adults, we're capable of understanding when our brains are being manipulated by the various platforms that make up the social media landscape, but even for adults, understanding the science of dopamine addiction can be difficult. How can we expect young, impressionable girls who are grappling with self-confidence issues daily to navigate this?

It's essential to ensure that our girls don't base their happiness on the number of likes their latest selfie or TikTok video received. How can we protect our pre-teen girls from the more negative aspects of social media to help ensure that they don't equate number of followers with self-worth?

This question raises devastating alarm bells about girls' increasing need to seek external validation. This phenomenon is explored in detail in the eye-opening Netflix documentary *The Social Dilemma*. It uses a combination of dramatised stories and professional commentary from industry insiders to reveal the dangers of social media. One of the most alarming comments was from social psychologist Dr Jonathan David Haidt, who teaches at NYU's Stern School of Business. He showcased a recent study on hospital admissions related to depression and anxiety in American teenage girls.

In 2010, when social media began to explode in popularity on mobile phones, rates of self-harm and suicide in girls began to rise. Rates for girls aged fifteen to eighteen were up by 62% while rates for girls aged ten to fourteen were up a shocking 189% between 2010 and 2015. That's nearly triple in just five years.[5]

Similarly, a 2017 study of NHS data found a 68% rise in hospital admissions for self-harm by teenage girls in the UK under the age of seventeen over the previous decade. The rate of hospitalisations for boys for the same cause has gone up by only 26% in the same amount of time.[6]

No one knows definitively why girls are more affected by social media than boys. One reason could be the comparisons of social standing and physical appearance that are more prevalent within young female relationships. Many of us have heard these facts before, and the association between self-esteem and external validation through social media isn't new. What is shocking is that we haven't sufficiently equipped our young teen girls to deal with the enormous health risks of this.

Pressures and expectations set by the media must change, and we must unlearn the standards of beauty that have been set for us. I recently discussed global beauty standards with one of my insightful podcast guests, the author Katherine Rundell.[7] She grew up on two different continents (Africa and Europe) and discovered as a young pre-teen that there seemed to be a narrow tightrope of acceptability for girls in their teen years. Her experience in different regions taught her that this tightrope changes from country to country.

This observation led her to conclude that there cannot and should not be only one way of thinking about and defining beauty. We must encourage our girls to hunt inside themselves and find their own version, while trying to get them to defy suggestions regarding what their face or body should look like. Since these standards are often set by those looking to prey on the insecurities of pre-adolescent girls, it's so important to help our girls understand that the beauty that matters most is that found within them.

Also worthy of consideration is how busy our girls are today. This only gets more problematic as they get older. Long, tiring days at school are followed by hobbies and sometimes more schooling. To unwind, they head to their social media platforms. Many teens are simply too busy and over-scheduled for frequent in-person interactions.[8]

To keep our youth connected to each other in real life rather than on social media, we need to help them strike a better balance between their schoolwork, hobbies and other lessons. Time to relax and have fun with friends is so important for young people, especially as they enter their teen years and become responsible for scheduling their own social time.

Working with social media

Like it or not, social media is a key part of the teen ecosystem. It's not going away, so either we get on board or we lose out. It can be a useful resource for education, connection and fun if we let it be. Helping our girls discover healthy ways to balance social media with real life, rather than banning it, should be our priority.

The digital world offers three main benefits, and they've been especially important during this global pandemic: connection, acceptance and support. Young people who normally feel isolated at school or alienated in social situations can find comfort in groups online. Social media platforms help them stay connected and enable them to explore communities where they feel accepted and supported. Social media isn't inherently good or bad. It's all in how it's used. Instead of hiding from it, we must embrace it and equip our youth with ways to use it to their advantage.

My top tip for parents is to set up a 'contract' with your tweens. This will help them feel as though you're engaging as equals and will allow you to set clear expectations about social media use right from the start. The contract needs to cover your agreed-upon terms for accessing their device and what they're allowed to do while they're on it. I suggest laying out your contract formally after having open, honest negotiations. You can type it up, enlarge it into a poster and make it visible in the house.

When it comes to apps, it's best to try to stay abreast of what's available, even if your tween isn't yet interested or legally able to access the most popular ones. There's an overwhelming number of apps out there, so it helps to be knowledgeable of the legal ages, benefits and disadvantages of each. That way you can be informed before your teen expresses interest in logging on.

Adolescent girls need to believe there will be real consequences for not sticking to the contract. These consequences should be agreed upon ahead of time. Deciding on these is just as important as the terms of the contract. If you take away her phone but she needs it to call an Uber to get to her sports match, this consequence won't be effective.

It's important to be purposeful and careful when choosing consequences. They'll be unique depending on the family and the situation but could include:

- Restricting her internet usage at home to school-related sites

- Replacing her phone with a model without internet access

- Prohibiting social media use for a set period

Once the terms of the contract have been decided, following through becomes crucial. It may be hard for some parents at first, but it's worth it in the long run. After coming to an agreement on acceptable apps, it's a good idea for parents to download them and add their child so they can check in on their activity.

Support and accountability are important as girls begin their online journey.

It's also essential to remind our girls that everything they share through texts and social media, even the 'disappearing' content on platforms such as Snapchat, can be seen by anyone. Social media is like an ongoing press conference after a big game. Your girl has been handed the microphone, and the world is potentially her audience.

The youth of today can change our future for the better. We're already seeing today's youth beginning to rectify the mistakes of previous generations. If we start from a place of positivity and optimism and equip them with knowledge of social media instead of simply banning it outright, it can become a useful tool. Consider the Black Lives Matter and climate change movements. These social movements illustrate how many benefits can be gained from engaging with online platforms.

Fashion and luxury expert Anita Balchandani of McKinsey & Company states that Gen Z is 'more reassuringly seeking out influencer culture that is meaningful and purpose driven. As a result, social media is moving away from a numbers game to a quality game.'[9] This outlook displays the hopeful beginnings of a potential cultural awakening.

Social media can also lead to some fun times as a family. I know from personal experience that girls will cringe, especially at first, if you try to join them in a TikTok video, but go with it and allow them to have a laugh at your expense. It can be a great bonding experience. Another way to connect with your daughter on social media is to send her accounts or news articles related to her passions and hobbies. This will reinforce your respect for her interests. Usually, she'll be pleased you did so, even if she doesn't show it. Your showing an interest in her life means a lot.

Persuade girls to share whatever it is they like to do on social media. If they're dancers, gymnasts or can help get cleaner water to impoverished areas through coding, encourage them to share this on social media. It's not a bad thing for kids to post memes or pictures of bubble tea, but we should always be encouraging our girls to share their authentic selves. Authenticity can inspire others – maybe they discovered a new bike trail, participated in a charity event, or finally landed a back flip. Our girls should also be encouraged to combat cyberbullying by shutting down bullies and building up their victims.

Before they log in

Preparing our girls for the online world requires some work on our part. We need to speak to them about how, unfortunately, some of our fellow humans aren't always kind and may have hurtful things to say about their posts. There's also the very real fear of missing out (FOMO) that is amplified when girls engage in a world where everyone is displaying what they're up to socially. It's important to be aware that many young teens hide their more explicit posts and comments by creating multiple accounts and hiding their more mature ones from their parents. To head this off before it happens, explicitly explain to your daughter that you wish to build trust with them, and share your hope that they can be honest with you about their behaviour on social media. Parents can also perform occasional spot checks on their daughters' browser histories, which will give them an indication of areas where more guidance may be needed.

Each family has its own moral compass. How we navigate our own rules is highly personal. Your daughter should have a clear understanding of the rules and norms around acceptable internet use within her own family, while also understanding that what matters to one family may not matter to another. Your family rules might be different from her best friend's, and that's okay. These rules may include time limits on device usage.

Explain to your daughter that switching off and tuning out to be with herself is an important part of accepting who she is. There's immense value in taking time away from screens to unwind, away from constant pings and notifications.

Teens and tweens are happiest when connecting with others, but this isn't necessarily healthy in extreme doses. Independence around social media usage is important, but an agreement on a realistic, healthy balance is essential. Though it may not always seem like it, teen girls thrive on boundaries and need parents and carers to set those for them. It's their role to push and the parent's role to find the correct balance.

Redefining happiness

Grumpy. Lazy. Annoyed. Irritated. Self-absorbed. Emotional.

If these descriptors ring true for you in terms of pre-adolescent teen girls, well, you're not alone. For many parents who are raising teen girls, 'happy' and 'content' aren't terms that come to mind when describing their offspring. This may be unsurprising, considering the immense changes in development, academic pressures and new social avenues that they're navigating every day. It's overwhelming and daunting, to say the least.

Ensuring teen girls are happy has never been more important. Bullying and societal pressures have risen to new heights thanks to the impossible standards that social media has set. It's all too easy not to celebrate individuality. Often, girls in their pre-teen and teen years can keep it together and appear quite self-assured or even happy at school. Once back in the comfort of their own homes, however, the effort of keeping up appearances can be too exhausting to maintain. This is why parents so often see the worst of their children.

We might ask why our once-sweet, lovely and pleasant daughters become so challenging during preadolescence. Instead, we should ask why we expect our daughters to be happy-go-lucky, knowing that the stress they're under is so enormous.

The benefits of a happy adolescence transcend the teenage years. A study conducted by University College London and the University of Warwick found that happy teens reported higher incomes as adults. Their study found that happy individuals' greater wealth is due, in part, to the fact that happy people are more likely to get a degree, find work and get promoted quicker than their gloomier counterparts.[10]

Teenagers can be happy in the right situations. To help our teen girls experience the happiness that's so important for their future well-being, we need to foster these situations as often as we can while measuring what really matters. It's easy to spend far too much time and energy worrying about outcomes for our girls that may not be that beneficial in the long run.

A role model in this area of my life is engineer Mo Gawdat, who explains that 'happiness happens when life seems to be going *your* way'.[11] That is, we feel happy when life behaves the way *we* want it to. He adds the caveat that it isn't actually the events that cause the happiness – rather, it's the way we think about them. We can teach our teens that we cannot control all the situations occurring around us, but we can control our actions and attitudes around those situations, and that this is all we can control. If we choose to sit in suffering because our expectations weren't met, then feelings of unhappiness are sure to take over. As parents, we can help our youngsters navigate expectations accordingly. This may be challenging because at this stage, their brains are inherently wired to think the worst of most situations.

Many ways to help foster happy teens are discussed in the following chapters as we go through the five-step methodology in greater detail. Both parents and educators can help girls experience more happiness with the strategies and tools suggested, but also by helping them understand that their expectations have a lot to do with their happiness. This goes for adults as well. We often equate success with results and outcomes from our own childhood and hold our girls up to impossible standards based on our expectations, not their reality.

Allowing time for your daughters to sit with their emotions (see Chapter Four) is a healthy route to getting them back to happiness. As parents, we often try to solve their problems and offer solutions, not realising that this can be motivated by our own anxieties. Our daughters just need us to listen. Providing them this space and teaching them to lean into their feelings will better enable them to move on after reaching a point of acceptance.

It can be difficult for them to open up about private matters to their parents. We desperately yearn to protect them from making impulsive decisions, but we need to give them this space to be themselves and to work out issues on their own.

A girl's teenage years will stay with her for the rest of her life. Adults who can barely recall events from two weeks ago can vividly recount times of true happiness or deep unhappiness that occurred when they were teenagers. Our aim here is to fill our girls' memories with as much of the former as possible.

While there's no doubt that adolescence can be difficult at times, there's also ample data to suggest that it can be a time of creativity, compassion and happy connections to adults and peers.

Importance of mentorship and role modelling

On 20 January 2021, the world watched in excitement and joy as Kamala Devi Harris became the first woman elected as vice president of the United States. Her election was boundary-breaking in several ways. Not only is she the first woman to hold the position, but she's also the first person of both African American and South Asian heritage to do so.

Vice President Harris is a remarkable public servant and community leader, having spent decades fighting for the rights of California's most vulnerable citizens as a prosecutor, district attorney, attorney general and senator.[12]

When people in leadership positions look like them, it's much easier for children to imagine that they too could one day hold similar positions. A wealth of research suggests that role modelling isn't just a matter of optics. It's a legitimate teaching tool that helps tackle both multiple biases, such as defining certain subjects as more suitable for one gender or another, and aspects of learning from new and diverse perspectives.

In one study of physicians' role modelling in education, the authors found that 'doctors historically have patterned their activities on those of practitioners whom they respect and trust. These have been called role models, "individuals admired for their ways of being and acting as professionals." Both consciously and unconsciously, we model our activities on such individuals.'[13]

Any teacher will tell you that there's more to education than just presenting the material and expecting
students to learn and understand it immediately.
Some of the most influential teachers are those who
can make the subject matter personal for each student.
This begins with an understanding of not just the
material but also how their presentation, personality
and style affect their students.

It's important for all female students to have role models who look like them, especially in STEM subjects
and other areas that have traditionally been bastions
of white male success.[14] A strong woman of colour
leading from the White House is a great first step, but
having mentors and role models closer to home is key
to helping our girls succeed.

One of the barriers holding girls back from STEM
fields, particularly, is the notable lack of role models. Most school-aged children know about Albert
Einstein and Thomas Edison, but they may not
have heard of Marie Curie, Sally Ride or Katherine
Johnson. Incorporating positive role models such as
these accomplished women into classes is a great way
to inspire students and encourage them to see themselves within these fields. There are many wonderful
books that showcase the history and accomplishments
of these remarkable role models.

Mentorship and role modelling are both positive
ways to inspire young learners, but to get them truly

engaged we need to help them find peers with similar interests, whether through in-person clubs or moderated online forums, for example. Networks can help young girls build the connections that will support them through their interests, and in their careers.

It's important to note that role models don't necessarily have to be people who look exactly like us. Individuals from underrepresented groups or people who have experienced barriers of some kind all make great role models for our young students.

Key points to land on

We must be careful and thoughtful when considering the many factors that lead to our daughters' happiness and success. Teen girls often face myriad complexities that are all quite new at this stage. One of the best things a parent can do is learn how to recognise and celebrate the many wonderful things about their daughter. Even if you feel that she knows and understands her good qualities, reiterating them until she truly believes in herself is so important. Addressing her concerns and finding the source of her worries is also key to unlocking her potential.

Additionally, parents must put in place helpful boundaries, especially around social media. We must also help our daughters maintain realistic expectations around many situations in life. The presence of positive role models can help show them the true meaning of happiness. It's critical to educate our girls at this pivotal and vulnerable stage of their growth to provide them with a solid foundation as they transition from childhood to adulthood.

Your daughter's childhood will pass all too quickly. Even if at times the days seem long, the years are short. Don't spend these special years fretting about your failings as a parent. This is your reminder that your daughter's happiness really depends on your being present and there for her – unconditionally.

TWO
Confidence

Before taking off

What do we mean when we ask our kids to be more confident? There's a healthy balance between coming across as arrogant or egotistical and being too nervous to voice our concerns or feelings. Finding this balance isn't always easy. We want our girls to be self-assured, but how can we teach them to be this way if they've had their confidence knocked?

There are countless barriers to our daughters' success. Among the most common is lack of confidence, which is why it is the first step in my five-step methodology. Confidence issues are far more likely to present themselves in girls than in their male peers in the impressionable pre-adolescent years. This chapter explores strategies to better support our girls to look inwards to accept themselves for who they are and find what makes them unique.

Building confidence begins by highlighting and celebrating all their incredible achievements, big or small. Often, girls don't believe that there's much in them to celebrate. We'll look at how we can create opportunities to point out their achievements. Our girls will begin to see these wins as well, and the cycle of comparison to others will begin to fade. Confidence is built when we learn to not just accept but also love ourselves.

Growth mindset: the power of the mind

Self-belief begins by helping girls shift the way they think. It's about fostering a growth mindset. With a growth mindset, they can see their inner voice as a force of championship. If we teach girls to change the language around their built-in thought patterns, they can take a new approach to challenges and feed messages to their brain that contain greater optimism and less self-doubt.

Children's brains go through a massive growth spurt when they're very young. By the time they're six, their brains are already about 90% to 95% the size of an adult's.[15] The brain still needs a lot of remodelling before it can function as an adult brain, though.

This remodelling happens intensively during adolescence and into a person's mid-twenties. Brain change depends on age, experience, and hormonal changes in puberty.[16] Most science curricula teach kids about the brain's chemical make-up and how it works. Some schools even teach growth mindset vs fixed mindset, a concept that was popularised by psychologist Carol Dweck.[17] Anyone, regardless of whether they're an adult or a child, can benefit from learning about the growth mindset.

A growth mindset involves thinking of the various aspects of yourself (your knowledge, personality traits, qualities, etc) as things that are changeable rather than fixed. If we believe that the hand we were dealt at birth is simply a starting place, it's a lot easier to change, evolve and grow. People who go through life with a fixed mindset are much more tempted to hide their deficiencies and make choices that validate the beliefs they already hold about themselves.

MATHTASTIC BRAIN FREEZE

Let's look at Esme, a twelve-year-old who throughout her primary school years was a secure and happy student in all areas – except maths. Despite being an able mathematician, she had extreme paranoia around the subject and found herself in extreme angst when faced with a maths test. Her panic would lead her to make careless errors, and she never left herself enough time to look over her answers. This resulted in scores that only cemented her belief that she was no good at maths. Though her *ability* was perfectly fine, her *test-taking skills* weren't at their best (yet). Years of subpar test results solidified for her that she was rubbish at maths and led her to believe that it was never a subject in which she could excel.

I began working with Esme to untangle this false belief. I explained to her that even if her beliefs regarding her ability were accurate, there were ways to strengthen her knowledge in the subject area. I also explained to her that her actual understanding of the concepts was what determined whether she was good at maths, not the test scores.

At first, she didn't want to believe it. I worked with her to instil the understanding that test-taking was simply a skill that perhaps she wasn't great at – *yet!* That key word, *yet*, is what all girls need to hear reinforced.

Esme had seen her peers, particularly boys in her class, relay solutions to maths problems with ease and proficiency. She allowed this and her test scores to serve as the evidence from which she drew her conclusion that she was a failure in this subject, so we mapped out a plan on how to improve test-taking skills. We spoke about how we could strengthen her brain's neurological pathways in a way that would help her take tests more efficiently to ensure she could maximise her scores. We also practised using language that reinforced her ability to do maths well and that spoke to improving her results. It was about avoiding statements such as, 'I'm a failure at maths'; 'It's too hard to do maths'; and 'It's not for me because I have more of a creative brain'. We looked at ways maths was also creative, which took her by surprise.

Once we started using timers and celebrating the number of questions she completed before each timer went off, she began to see that her ability in the subject was better than she'd let herself believe. Next, we spoke about solving questions worth the most marks and perhaps starting with those and then ending the test with the remaining questions. The idea that she didn't have to complete the test in the order it was written also took her by surprise. She was used to just doing things the way one does when reading a book and never questioned it.

It will come as no surprise that the more she did this and continued to build the right messages around her self-talk, the more her test scores improved. Eventually, she became so much better at achieving high results that her teacher asked her if she was finding the set she was in too easy and suggested moving her into a faster-paced one. This fuelled her self-belief, and Esme worked even harder to prove to herself that she could keep up with her peers in a more advanced maths set. The evidence now seemed to point to the fact that she was indeed a good mathematician and that, as a result of practising and working on strategies with a growth mindset, she was also a great maths test-taker.

Esme isn't a unique case, particularly when it comes to this subject. Far too often, I hear young girls say that maths isn't for them, or that it isn't made for the female brain. They allow themselves to think that because they aren't as fast as their male peers or able to solve the questions under timed pressure that they must be less adequate. This is simply not the case. We must do better at watching what signals we provide to girls around subjects such as maths and science. There are far too few girls in STEM subjects due to a lack of belief in themselves.

Many young people assume that most scientists are men because of what they've seen historically and in the media. It's important to counter that assumption. Parents can foster a growth mindset in their daughters by emphasising that practice improves performance. Everywhere we look, there are subtle and unsubtle messages telling our girls that STEM subjects aren't 'for them'. One study of movies revealed that only 11.6% of characters with a STEM job were played by women.[18] In most blockbuster films and TV shows, the scientists, mathematicians, engineers and researchers are played by men.

Furthermore, as a society, we've made major assumptions about who performs best in subjects such as maths and science. This bias, however unconscious, has led to academic and financial support being drawn away from certain groups and given to those whom we believe to be more adept in these subjects. Unequal distribution of financial and academic support has a much larger impact on performance than each student's raw aptitude does. It has profound implications for lower-income students, and particularly girls from visible minority groups.

We all understand that there are many complexities surrounding a child's development and brain formation, which continues until around the age of twenty-five.[19] As parents, though, we don't always realise that issues of brain development and processing aren't always within our child's control. It's not fair to blame them for failing to make valid connections when their brain is still developing, while also remembering to look back and celebrate the progress already made.

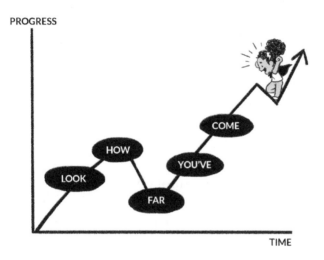

Neuroplasticity and the power of positive thought patterns

In the midst of grief over the tragic loss of his son, Ali, Mo Gawdat tested a new algorithm – one that would change the trajectory of his life and work. As a tribute to Ali, Gawdat made it his life's mission to help others 'solve for happiness'.

Drawing on his background in engineering and mathematics, he has worked to understand and explore many of the myths regarding happiness. He's put his considerable talents and intelligence into helping others engineer their minds towards happiness by managing and preventing disappointment.

After reading his book *Solve for Happy: Engineer Your Path to Joy*[20] and having the privilege of speaking to Mo on my podcast,[21] I reconfirmed that the best way to empower our youth is to help them understand their relationship to the brain, which is truly the most incredible organ. The more we can change and develop our mindset, the greater the potential for happiness.

Too many people go through life holding the belief that their brains cannot be changed. The truth is our brains are much more plastic (capable of growth and change) than we give them credit for. Our brains can change their physical structure and functional organisation – an ability that's formally known as 'neuroplasticity'.

Forming new neural connections, strengthening existing connections, and even growing new neurons is possible through training and experience. These new and improved neural connections are what increase our capacity for both learning and growth.[22] One researcher and lecturer who has been central in the study of neuroplasticity is Barbara Arrowsmith-Young.

At a young age, she realised that she had severe learning difficulties that made everything from reading to mathematics a challenge. She worked diligently to develop exercises she could practise to improve her capacity for learning. In 1980, she opened the Arrowsmith School and brought students in with the goal of changing the 'capacity of the learner to learn so that the learner can understand, absorb, retain, process and use the content, laying the foundation for learning'. She proved to herself that she could find ways to remove the blocks in the wiring of the neurological connections within her brain. She explains this in greater detail on The Elevate Podcast for anyone looking for more information on her work.[23]

Going through life with a fixed mindset that's closed to the possibilities of growth and change is incredibly damaging. With some effort, we can use our brains as a force for positive change. Instead of getting caught up in negative thoughts, we must focus on engaging our brain in a more positive way. The more we practise silencing our inner critic, the more we'll be able to make meaningful, positive changes in our lives. Thinking of your brain as something within your control often helps quiet the inner critical voice and gives you more space to be your own cheerleader.

Small talk, big issues

When our son was almost three years old, my husband and I took him to see the top neurologist in our hometown of London. Despite having reached many other milestones, he still wasn't speaking. We weren't overly concerned about this and assumed that the stories we'd been told about boys being later talkers were true.

My husband's hunch that there might be an underlying issue had led us to seek speech therapy. After spending time with our son, the speech therapist wasn't concerned but encouraged us to see a physician to put our minds to rest and rule out any sinister possibilities. Feeling certain we were visiting the doctor only for precautionary reasons, I nonchalantly and ambivalently proceeded to the appointment on my own with our son, unaware of what I was in for that morning – a huge punch to my core. It knocked me over sideways (quite literally).

The doctor conducted her assessment in a matter-of-fact manner. Then, at the end of two long hours, she sat me down and suggested that we ought to consider the possibility our son might be the A word – autistic. Full disclosure: this was a word I'd only ever associated with the movie *Rain Man*. The word terrified me, as I was so ill prepared for the possibility that our son might have a life different to the one I'd already mapped out to mirror his big sister's. Through my streaming tears, I could muster only, 'What does that even mean? I mean, will he *ever* talk?'

The doctor, lacking bedside manner to say the least, coldly replied, 'I don't know. We can only hope.'

Hope? Only hope? It wasn't the answer any mother wants to hear. I'd wanted to hear her say it would all be fine if we just did x, y and z. She didn't say this. There were no ifs, buts or maybes, even though every cell in my body was pleading for her to say something, anything else. I managed to splutter another question. 'What does that mean – I mean, for his future?'

Her response, which still haunts me, was loud and clear. 'Well, he'll probably get a great job in IT or computer programming, and as he's such a handsome fellow, I feel certain a lovely young lady will want to be with him. A nice nurse would be so good.'

You must be thinking that I'm making this up. That no doctor would tell their patient something based on so many ill-informed stereotypes. I promise you I'm not. What followed days of sadness, worry and a shedload of tears was a journey to not rely solely on hope but to use science to change our son's wiring around speech. We vowed to work as hard as we possibly could to get him communicating.

I picked myself up, read all about the brain's ability to change and enlisted the help of a supportive and hardworking speech therapist who specialised in children with autism-related speech concerns. Along with the hours in clinic with his therapists, my husband and I worked day and night to teach my son the mechanisms on how to train his brain. We practised ways to move the correct muscles in his oral cavity to make the sounds necessary to speak.

As it transpired, my son (like many neurodiverse children) had multiple concerns and learning challenges, known as comorbidities. He was later diagnosed with verbal dyspraxia as well as autism. We went from sounds to blending letters, and just before he turned five, he said his first words. It's a moment that I'll never forget.

Today, he speaks in full sentences, sings beautifully and sometimes even raps the lyrics to his favourite grime tracks. He's also reading books with simple text. Is he the best communicator or the most articulate child around? No, but his story shows that the brain can be trained. It's a malleable organ that has an extraordinary ability to alter and shift. Of course, I'll never really know if my merely hoping for his speech to transpire might have worked out in due course, but something tells me that if hope on its own was enough, many children's lives would look very different. I also appreciate the huge amount of privilege my son's story contains. He has two parents with the means to afford extra support, and access to resources many children do not. This isn't something I ever take for granted, and it fuels my passion to keep working on ways to advocate for, support and mentor others, especially young girls.

All children with learning challenges are unique

It's important to debunk some of the current stereotypes, such as the one mentioned by our doctor, around additional needs. Every person with learning challenges presents differently. Taking steps to dismantle myths about the most common learning differences will better equip us to appreciate that all children with learning challenges are unique and shouldn't be painted with the same brush.

It's essential to offer each child appropriate support and understanding. Otherwise, youth with learning disabilities can end up setting low expectations for themselves. It's then easy for them to become apathetic about their education, or worse, their future. Research and evidence-based instruction regarding learning difficulties has progressed a great deal over the last few years, but our general knowledge and perception of learning difficulties hasn't. Gaining a more accurate understanding of the wide spectrum of these issues will help our community immeasurably.

Many learning disabilities are invisible, which makes it difficult for parents and teachers to understand how and why a child might be struggling. This contributes to widely held views about the different ways students exhibit behaviours, or cope with their diagnoses. It's rare for two girls with the same diagnosis to endure challenges in exactly the same way, so it's essential to examine some of the most common stigmas attributed to youth once they've been given a label or a diagnosis.

The stigmas that have been attached to these diagnoses over the years have had a deeply negative effect on both parents and children. Whether your child exhibits these common traits or not, it's important to understand that every child is different. We should never make assumptions based on the most common denominator. The stigmas and stereotypes attached to youth with learning challenges can most likely be attributed to societal realities. There's a significant and stubborn part of our population that believes learning differences are simply excuses for laziness and poor parenting and seeks to push them out of the realm of 'acceptable' conditions.

When the dark clouds of doom and gloom associated with stigmas and stereotypes are lifted, students can capitalise on their strengths. Most importantly, we must remember that one way of learning isn't 'right', or better than another. Brains are wired differently, and when we can accept this, we can provide greater space for our youth with learning differences to let their own light shine.

Body confidence

Many women of all ages lack body confidence, and young girls are no exception. Girls often put themselves down because they don't feel pretty enough. It's important to recognise that it isn't just the beauty industry setting high standards but also the girls themselves. Today's young people are often referred to as 'Generation Selfie' and are more likely than previous generations to have low self-esteem because of social media.

Both internal and external beauty standards can lead girls to tell themselves the following:

• 'You're not good enough as you are.'

• 'You need to be lighter, thinner, taller, etc.'

• 'You're cute, but not as pretty as your friends.'

The pre-adolescent years, starting at the age of eight, are the most formative when it comes to girls' self-esteem.[24] Research indicates that self-esteem increases rapidly from this time into adolescence then gradually begins to slow its growth curve as adolescents transition into early adulthood. These years are also when many young girls learn about and embrace beauty standards in many forms, including colourism.[25]

While the effects of social media on self-esteem are well-documented, concerns over the impact of retouching apps and filters are only just starting to emerge. These apps encourage girls to stare intently – and critically – at their own reflection. Disturbingly, instead of being encouraged to admire their perfect imperfections, they're given digital tools to 'fix' them. They can play around with their features until they're unrecognisable.

We must remind our girls of their inner and outer beauty, but a larger, more urgent task lies in moving away from conventional beauty standards. We have entirely normalised obsessing over body shape and size, in everything from media and film to fashion and advertising.[26] The more our girls are exposed to these standards, the thinner their ideal body shape, and the more likely it is that they'll experience disordered eating.

A good way to combat unrealistic beauty standards is to promote the idea that beauty shines from within. Focusing on character traits, such as kindness, loyalty, patience and compassion will help build our daughters' self-esteems, so they're less susceptible to toxic messaging in advertising and media. It's also important to present girls with diversity and variety in beauty. Many companies have made both token and sincere efforts towards diversity since the Black Lives Matter movement of 2020, but in the vast landscape of media and advertising, inclusion remains slow-going.

It's still difficult for girls of diverse backgrounds to turn on the TV and see someone who looks like them. This is largely due to the absence of representation. Girls are left to wonder where they fit in and why others with similar features remain largely unrepresented. If they don't see themselves represented, girls naturally begin to assume that they could never be considered 'beautiful' looking the way they do. We need to see greater representation within the role models of society, to help make girls feel like they belong. When girls don't feel good about the way they look, they're more likely not to take part in activities or opportunities.[27]

Encourage girls to open up to each other about beauty standards on shape, colour, size, age and disabilities as these conversations can help boost a girl's self-esteem for a lifetime. I have students asking me why, for example, even kids' clothing campaigns don't include girl models with braces or glasses more regularly. Using girls with more realistic traits would make campaigns much more relatable. These conversations are also part of a much wider strategy that will ultimately empower teachers, parents and young people to understand the nuances of conventional beauty standards and the social pressures that enforce them. Additionally, the gatekeepers within this industry must engage more deeply with the conscious and unconscious messaging within their projects.

Dove and Gucci campaigns

A brilliant example of a company working to combat these falsified, inflated and unrealistic standards of beauty is Dove. It has renewed its fight against unrealistic beauty standards with campaigns that highlight the damage caused by heavily edited selfies on social media.

Alessandro Manfredi, Dove's executive vice president, says, 'Now that social media has grown to be part of our everyday lives, digital distortion is happening more than ever and tools once only available to the professionals can be accessed by young girls at the touch of a button without regulation... Girls all around the world have begun to feel the pressure to edit and distort how they look, to create something "perfect", which cannot be achieved in real life.'[28]

Dove hopes to start a movement to build confidence with the hashtag #NoDigitalDistortion and will be running ads all over the world. They've also put their considerable resources towards the Dove Self-Esteem Project. Through partnerships with world-renowned academics, doctors, psychologists and more, the project aims to offer resources to parents, educators and youth leaders on how they can 'help young people form healthy friendships, overcome body image issues and be their best selves'.[29]

Their goal is to engage with 250 million young people by 2030. With more than 60 million young people reached so far, they're already on the right path. Ideally, they can reach young people at a critical juncture in their lives, when 44% of girls are trying to lose weight[30] and 75% of girls with low self-esteem are engaging in harmful activities such as cutting, smoking, drinking or bullying as a way to deal with their feelings of low self-worth.[31]

Another company that has been making a concerted effort to improve representation within their brand is Gucci. The luxury retailer recently hired seventeen-year-old Ellie Goldstein, a model who has Down's syndrome. 'It feels so amazing and fabulous to be part of the Gucci Beauty campaign,' Goldstein told *British Vogue*. 'I feel so proud of myself, especially to have been chosen for this.'[32]

Ellie's debut coincides with Gucci Beauty's Unconventional Beauty campaign, an initiative launched during the PhotoVogue Festival on Instagram in 2020. Ellie, along with other models representing many beautifully diverse populations, was photographed for a *Vogue Italia* editorial after being scouted for the project on Instagram.[33]

It's imperative that more companies use their online platform to shift the dialogue around what's considered beautiful. If media representation doesn't continue to expand to reflect the diversity in the world around us, the mental health repercussions will be severe. After all, our girls' self-esteem is much more related to their views on beauty than the physical reality of their shape and size. Too often, young girls get trapped in a cycle of disordered eating when they aren't feeling secure about themselves.

But first, love yourself

So many celebrities and influencers use their platforms to showcase ideas around self-care – the best new way to exfoliate, eat, bathe or just breathe. Many people now loathe the term 'self-care', associating it with expensive creams or lavish days at the spa. At its core, though, self-care is self-love. It doesn't mean you must spend hours soaking in a bath (though you're most welcome to do so). It means carving out time in the day to look after yourself. Self-care doesn't need to be time-consuming, physically draining or costly. Sometimes it's the quick, simple things that happen regularly that rejuvenate us, like watching your favourite film, going out for walk, drawing or writing in your journal.

Self-care is important for everyone. It allows us to feel and be our best, and it can have profound effects on our self-esteem. When we take care of ourselves, we affirm our self-worth. By encouraging girls to take time for themselves, we're telling them that they deserve it, and they do. With the right role modelling and understanding of what makes us truly happy, we can work towards resolving the many inevitable bumps of teen years.

Disordered eating

One of the most devastating experiences a tween girl can endure is an eating disorder. In this period of a girl's development, it doesn't take much for an intense focus on appearance to turn into something more sinister. Although it's still relatively uncommon for girls in the tween years to experience eating disorders, many individuals who develop serious eating disorders, such as bulimia and anorexia nervosa, start showing clear symptoms around this age. Teens and adolescents are also more likely to develop avoidant/restrictive food intake disorder (ARFID), which encompasses any sort of restrictive or avoidant behaviour around food or eating.[34] Preliminary research suggests that ARFID may affect up to 5% of children.[35]

Add the fact that many tweens profess a desire to be thinner and often associate being thin with being attractive and well-liked and it's easy to understand why girls may feel pulled into disordered eating. A lot of scholarship has gone into determining why some girls are more vulnerable to eating disorders, and why they develop them at such a young age. Culture and personality are two of the main drivers.

There are many ways that culture can affect our girls' perception of their bodies. Even positive, well-meaning messaging on diet, exercise and body image can begin to have a negative effect if girls hear it too often and are unable to understand that it's meant to be helpful. As well, many girls who have developmental or learning challenges are at increased risk for eating disorders. Anxiety, perfectionism, obsessive-compulsive tendencies and depression have been linked to the early development of eating disorders.[36]

If an eating disorder is left untreated, it can lead to serious medical issues that can easily impact a girl's development. Girls with eating disorders have also been found to be more likely to engage in other dangerous behaviours, such as suicidal ideation and self-harm. In one 2016 study, 60% of young female patients admitted to hospital for an eating disorder also displayed suicidal behaviour, while a further 49% showed symptoms of self-harm.[37]

It can be particularly difficult to spot the early warning signs of an eating disorder in tween girls because their hobbies, interests and behaviours are changing before our eyes. Many parents also find that their children start to become more aware of the world around them at this age, leading them to make choices that are distinct from those of other family members, such as being vegetarian or vegan.

Despite these challenges, doctors and researchers have isolated certain signs as being particularly troubling around this age. Here are a few important symptoms to be aware of:

- Skipping meals, or eating in secret

- An intense, unhealthy focus on healthy eating, or food in general

- Worrying about being fat

- Expressing disgust or shame about their eating habits

- Rapid weight loss[38]

Key points to land on

A growth mindset can radically alter confidence levels. Knowing the science behind how the brain can be wired differently will better enable young people (and adults, too) to take charge of elevating their self-belief. It's challenging to give pre-teens and teens orders on how to gain more confidence. If they understand and see the mechanisms on how to help themselves build it, they're much more likely to do the work.

Revealing how the brain is our power organ will help establish buy-in from otherwise sceptical adolescent youth. Helping them build confidence in their abilities and their physical self is the first crucial step in ensuring our girls are balanced, healthy and happy.

There are many reasons that contribute to a drop in our girls' confidence during adolescence, including the role the media plays in body positivity. The adverse effects of setting beauty standards at unattainable levels can have a huge impact on teen mental health, such as developing low self-esteem and eating disorders. The value in teaching girls about self-care and owning who they are should not be underestimated at this impressionable stage of their growth.

THREE
Empathy

Before taking off

Empathy is a skill that will stay with our girls for life. Being able to place oneself in another's shoes results in a greater understanding of the people we socialise, work and live with. This is especially critical in our cultivation of a more inclusive society. Empathy is the most important skill we need to relate to people of different abilities, ethnicities, ages, genders and much more.

Too many young girls ignore the importance of looking outwards to feel what another person is experiencing and understand their frame of reference. Instead, they're often more inwardly concerned. The adolescent years are a crucial time to learn about empathy.

This chapter explores ways to teach girls how to consider other points of view and become good listeners.

Learning perspectives

In the *Journal of Advanced Nursing*, nurse and researcher Theresa Wiseman defines the four attributes of empathy:

- To be able to see the world as others see it

- To be nonjudgemental

- To understand another person's feelings

- To communicate your understanding of that person's feelings[39]

The best way to teach empathy is by role modelling examples of it. Young people who see practical examples of empathy and collaboration with peers are likely to employ the same tactics. With collaboration, we create stronger communities and better ourselves. Teachers across all disciplines working together and exchanging ideas benefits not just the girls, but the adults around them as well.

As an educator, I believe that a multidisciplinary approach to teaching benefits all youngsters. It's key to allow students to tap into their senses through movement (kinesthetic learning), play (interactive), and auditory and visual means. For example, for girls with concentration concerns, movement breaks can improve their ability to maintain focus. The main class teacher could learn a few simple drills from the PE teacher and use these to give all their students a movement break (rather than singling one student out) after concentrated desk work. An act of collaboration like this one can make a huge impact on learning outcomes for pupils. It exhibits empathy for different learning styles.

It can be challenging to persuade people who are wrapped up in their beliefs to consider alternate points of view. In his recent book *Think Again*, organisational psychologist Adam Grant presents the idea that 'instead of trying to force other people to change, you're better off helping them find intrinsic motivation to do so'. He suggests interviewing others – in essence, asking open-ended questions and listening carefully then holding up a mirror so they can see their thoughts more clearly.[40] Empathy isn't about changing someone's mind so they agree with your point of view. It's about trying to understand another's way of thinking and asking them whether they might be open to some rethinking."

Girls in their tween and teen years can often seem closed-minded and self-absorbed. As their parents, our instinct might be to take the polar opposite stance in any given situation, but our going on the attack will only make our girls shut down or fight back harder.

Instead, we should be encouraging our girls to understand other points of view, including those held by their parents. If we preach about why we're right and they're wrong, it can backfire and strengthen the beliefs they already hold. As they develop, it's vital for us to continue to show them ways in which they can open their minds to new perspectives.

Here are some examples of phrases you can use:

- 'Is there a different way you could approach that?'
- 'Can you explain why you feel that way?'
- 'What makes you think that?'

Active listening

It's quite extraordinary how many times a day a young person might be asked by adults, 'Did you hear me?', 'Are you listening?', 'Why didn't you just listen the first time?' and countless other variations of this. Young folks may adopt the 'in one ear, out the other' philosophy due to the sheer volume of information they need to digest.

By teaching our girls skills around active listening, we can help them to develop the important skills around empathy. Active listening is part of the foundation of effective communication. It's also an essential ingredient in the development of crucial skills such as problem-solving, teamwork and leadership.

Active listening skills will help improve girls' experiences and relationships for the rest of their lives. Psychologists have found that when we listen carefully and call attention to the nuances in other people's thinking, they become less extreme and more open in their views.[41,42]

There are four types of listening:

1. Appreciative listening – primarily for enjoyment

2. Empathetic listening – for better understanding others and sharing mutual concerns

3. Comprehensive listening – for learning new concepts (for most of us, this requires the deepest levels of concentration)

4. Critical listening – for making important decisions (analysing and evaluating what you hear so you can come to an informed conclusion)[43]

It's worthwhile to note that auditory processing systems aren't fully developed until around the age of fourteen.[44] Teens may hear our words but take time to fully respond because they're still processing what we said. A 'huh?' doesn't necessarily indicate that they're ignoring you on purpose. It could be a sign that they need extra time to think and require patience from us.

This is of course the case when we're raising girls with learning challenges. Unfortunately, time seems to be the resource that most parents and educators lack due to all the demands they face in a day. We often find ourselves short of patience and ultimately exasperated when trying to display our own listening skills. We can work towards being better listeners by thinking about the following key elements of active listening:

- **Attentiveness**, which begins with good eye contact and attention to the speaker's body language.

- **Engagement**, which can be demonstrated with actions (such as a nod or a smile) and an open posture.

- **Feedback**, which in this case means asking questions, not offering solutions; it often requires withholding judgement, interruptions or counter arguments.

- **Responding** respectfully and honestly.

As author and inspirational speaker Simon Sinek explains, 'Hearing is listening to what is said. Listening is hearing what isn't said.'[45] It's important to pay attention not only to the words our girls speak, but also to the more discreet, subtle messages and cues they provide, whether through body language or changes in behaviour. This will give us a better understanding of what exactly our girls are hoping to communicate to us. Where and when we choose to speak with our girls can also have a considerable influence on how well they feel listened to or heard. It can be better to try to ascertain their true thoughts during car rides or walks or just before bedtime instead of right after they've come back from a party or day out, for example. Even with best intentions, the young can feel they are being interrogated or we are not respecting their privacy when we launch into a line of questioning as soon as they return home from being out. Instead, choose a time when they are more relaxed and at ease and more likely to accept you are asking from a place of care and concern, not being nosy or seen as 'annoying' them.

Many girls are articulate and well spoken but can struggle when it comes to voicing deeper concerns and thoughts. It can be difficult to lean into the massive, often messy mixture of questions, concerns and worries stirring inside them. Let's face it – emotions can be painful, and nobody wants to sit in pain or discomfort. It's in these moments of discomfort, though, where the greatest clarity on perspectives can be gained.

In her famous 2012 TED Talk 'Listening to Shame', Brené Brown says, 'If you put shame in a petri dish, it needs three ingredients to grow exponentially: secrecy, silence and judgement. If you put the same amount of shame in the petri dish and douse it with empathy, it can't survive.'[46] Illustrating to our daughters just how far they can go towards eradicating shame with the power of empathy is necessary.

Many young folks fail to recognise that some of their most isolating thoughts and experiences are also the most universal. If they're taught to share and express their thoughts in a meaningful way and to reach out for support when they need it, they'll receive empathy and begin to understand that they're not alone. Sharing isolating experiences helps normalise them. It's never been more important for parents to encourage mutually empathetic relationships with their daughters. If we don't model, teach and practise empathy, we risk raising girls who are self-obsessed or have a narrow-minded view of the world.

In *Daring Greatly*, Brown writes that when it comes to empathy, 'There is no script. There is no right way or wrong way to do it. It's simply listening, holding space, withholding judgement, emotionally connecting, and communicating that incredibly healing message of "You're not alone."'[47] For decades, Brown has researched the significance of empathy. She defines it as a skill and stresses the importance of actively practising giving and receiving empathy.[48] Being an empathetic, active listener for girls will provide them with the superpower of being able to build and foster happy, healthy social connections while learning to regulate their emotions.

Active listening may well begin in classrooms or at home, but the skill will take our girls well beyond these places into the world of work, travel, post-secondary education and adult relationships.

Empathy and effective leadership

Learning empathy at a young age will pay dividends. It has been correlated with higher academic achievement, better communication skills and a lower likelihood of getting involved in bullying.[49]

It's particularly apparent in our current polarised climate just how beneficial it is to be able to cultivate strong relationships with those who are different from us. This is especially important in professional situations. We've seen time and again that leaders who lead with empathy are more respected because they make decisions with great care and while looking through the eyes of others.

Since every situation is unique, it's important to equip our future leaders with the ability to pay attention to how people around them are feeling and take corresponding measures to support them. We want our girls to make a positive difference in people's lives.

As the COVID-19 pandemic unfolded, many female political leaders around the world gained acclaim for their clarity of communication, decisiveness and empathetic actions around the crisis. This praise came regardless of whether they were leading large or small nations, wealthy or poor ones, or land-locked or coastal ones.[50] They were able to show empathy and connect with citizens on a much deeper level, leading to more positive outcomes. This is what we want from our leaders during difficult situations.

Using empathy, leaders can let go of expectations, pressures and assumptions and encourage generative ideas to emerge. Positive psychology studies suggest that positive emotions allow individuals to broaden their horizons, promoting the discovery of new resources, ideas and actions. Neuroimaging studies show that compassion activates areas of the brain associated with learning and decision-making. Moreover, research on the effect of leaders' emotional intelligence shows that leaders' empathy towards their teams encourages team creativity.[51] By tapping into empathy, both for themselves and for others, leaders can foster an environment in which creativity and innovation can flourish, thus helping organisations build a better and kinder world.

Exploring empathy in the following ways can offer eye-opening results and help foster strong leadership.

- Get out of your usual environment and step into a new area for discovery, striking up conversations with people you meet along the way.

- Seek feedback from those you trust.

- Be curious and ask questions.

- Be honest and reflect on your own biases.

- Explore things with both the heart and the head.

Empathy in friendships

Tween and teen friendships are often challenging, and many girls grapple with the turbulence they can present. Growing up, every girl wishes to form friendships that are both fun and meaningful. It can be a struggle for girls to separate a true friend from someone who doesn't want the best for them, especially those who have learning, social and/or emotional difficulties that are making them feel inadequate.

As arduous as this may seem for our daughters, parents and carers should avoid stepping in to manage this aspect of their lives. While we need to teach them about healthy friendships, it's valuable to allow girls to arrive at conclusions on their own. Our goal should be to show them support and encourage their growth while demonstrating that the traits that make them different are worth celebrating. It's crucial to embolden our girls to celebrate differences within themselves and others and to use empathy to pursue better, healthier friendships.

One of the ways that children cope with the trials of pre-teen and adolescent years is by doing everything possible to fit in. If they have learning or social challenges, these differences can be a source of shame that causes low self-esteem, anxiety and stress. Instead of encouraging our girls to fit in, we should be working on ways for them to feel happy in themselves, so they can celebrate their differences with greater empathy. Here are some ways to do this:

- Normalise extra help and support sessions

- Reframe the way differences around race, gender and sexuality are discussed

- Help them develop a greater vocabulary to discuss their feelings

- Encourage them to demonstrate empathy for themselves as well as their peers

When girls are confident in themselves and what they can offer the world, it becomes easier for them to reach out and connect empathetically with others – empathy is necessary for a relationship to progress beyond the superficial. Simultaneously, we as parents and mentors must work to help instil in our daughters a positive, realistic view of friendship. We should never dictate whom they should be friends with, but we can help them understand the basic tenets of a good friendship.

Our girls need to see friendship as a positive element in their lives. Competition or a desire to be popular isn't a beneficial foundation for any relationship. Friendships built with one person at the centre will quickly lead to competition and infighting. As well, any sort of judgement in a relationship creates barriers, which lead to conflict, and conflict invariably precedes stress.

Just as empathy is essential to any friendship, so is trust. It's important that girls understand the importance of trusting the right people. An ability to trust with caution will allow girls to open up and be vulnerable with their friends, leading to deeper intimacy.

ZARA'S STORY

Here's an example of how empathy can help improve friendships. My student Zara has a hypermobility condition which makes it difficult for her to take part in team sports, be too daring on the playgrounds or even join birthday parties that require physical strength, such as those involving climbing or trampoline parks. She often feels excluded not just from the parties, but also from the inside jokes or discussions that her peers inevitably share after the event. Not having the sensitivity to understand that Zara might be feeling low about missing out, the other girls add to her misery by highlighting that the reason she missed out on the event was her health condition.

If these girls were taught about empathy, two actions could be taken that would create a different outcome. First, the girls could plan parties or play games that would allow more girls, including Zara, to attend. Second, the sharing of unrelatable and noninclusive anecdotes could take place less overtly.

The difficulty here is that we want to give the other girls the benefit of the doubt. Since Zara seems strong and has adapted well to her condition (at least on the surface), they may not realise that she's feeling much more hurt than she's letting on. This example portrays the value of making empathetic behaviour the outcome that should supersede any kind of guess work. That is, giving girls skills on empathy in a strong enough manner that they have the awareness to keep activities and conversations inclusive of all parties around. Being excluded is never a great feeling, but to be excluded because of a medical condition is extremely challenging for young girls. Showing empathy towards friends of all different backgrounds and situations has the power to make a profound impact.

Empathy and bullying

If healthy friendships are at one end of the spectrum, bullying is at the other. It's a sad reality so many of our youth are facing. Bullying happens most often during the tween years. An astounding 48% of children say that they've been bullied and have experienced the harassment, manipulation, ostracism and more that peaks between the ages of eleven and thirteen then thankfully begins to decline.[52]

With bullying extending its reach due to social media, it's never too early to talk to our girls about bullying. Even if your daughter isn't being actively bullied, making her aware of the problem can help her be more confident if she's ever targeted. It may also help her assist others in a situation where she's either part of a social group that's bullying others or she happens to witness bullying.

To help our girls understand bullying, we parents must first be aware of some of the critical differences between tween girls and tween boys when it comes to situations like these. Generally, boys are bullied less than their female classmates. Boys tend to be more physically aggressive and will attack or fight others to raise their status within a group. Male bullying in the schoolyard tends to end quickly, without either party holding a grudge. Boys in general are much more accepting of bullying behaviour, and may continue to be friends with their bullies, or those who bully others.

Comparatively, girls are much less likely to use physicality in their conflicts. Instead, they bully indirectly, through gossip, ostracism and other passive-aggressive methods. These techniques may seem less damaging in isolation but can wear away at a girl's self-esteem. In one study that analysed four years' worth of data from the Centers for Disease Control and Prevention's Youth Risk Behaviour Survey, researchers found that girls were more likely to be bullied and were also more likely to think about or even attempt suicide.[53] These two correlated figures are worrying.

To help protect girls from the dangers of bullying, we must help them gain the emotional and interpersonal skills necessary to thrive. We should also be nurturing in them a strong sense of self. Firstly, nurture empathy through open-mindedness around emotions. By speaking freely about emotions and raising children in an emotion-rich environment, you can help them feel more confident bringing up issues when they arise. Secondly, encourage their confidence. Both tween boys and girls find it easier to bully a child who has low self-esteem.[54] Helping girls gain confidence (as discussed in Chapter Two) will help them push back against bullies and will also make them less likely to become a bully themselves.

Almost everyone knows what it's like to witness bullying. It can make us feel helpless, frustrated and afraid, and these feelings stick with us long after we've grown up. Despite this, most of us still don't know what we'd do differently if we were put back into that schoolyard situation. To help our girls feel more confident and courageous than we felt in those moments, we must empower them to be upstanders.

Being a bystander is one of the easiest ways to handle conflict. A bystander is someone who simply doesn't get involved. Many of us may have been told that this is the preferable way to handle bullying, as it helps prevent furthering the conflict and minimises risk. There's a better approach. An upstander is an individual who puts themself at risk by coming to a victim's aid. Although the word 'upstander' wasn't added to the Oxford English Dictionary until 2016,[55] we've seen these individuals throughout history. They've been called guardian angels, good Samaritans, or, simply, leaders.

It's easier to be an upstander when you have a strong sense of self-worth and self-esteem. When a girl doesn't feel confident in herself, it's difficult for her to step out of her comfort zone and into an active bullying situation. Empowering our daughters to be upstanders starts by instilling in them a strong sense of self-worth. From there, we can help them develop their skills in empathy and teach them techniques that will help them move from bystander to upstander.

An upstander doesn't have to interrupt the conflict to lend a hand. While that approach can work, there are other ways to help, which is why it's important to teach our girls the nuances of being an upstander. If they're afraid of getting in the middle of a conflict, they can still be an upstanding friend by checking in with the victim privately after the bullying incident with an empathetic ear, supporting them if they wish to alert an adult about the situation, or mobilising others to stand up to the bully together.

Many people find it easier to confidently engage in a situation if they've thought about what they would say beforehand. We can help our girls be upstanding friends by working with them to determine what they could do or say when confronted with bullying. Here are some suggestions you could offer:

- 'Hey, I don't like how you're talking to my friend.'

- 'That's not a very nice thing to say.'

- 'I just saw that you were being bullied. Are you OK? Is there anything I can do to help?'

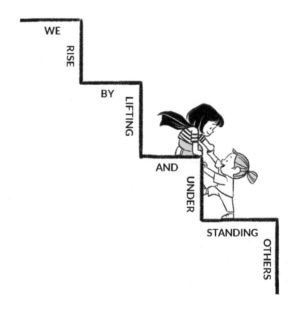

When your daughter is the culprit

One of the hardest parenting experiences out there is learning that your child is the perpetrator of bullying behaviour.

MAXINE'S STORY

Ten-year-old Maxine was a student I worked with who struggled with her friendships. One of the things holding her back from making friends was her craving of the limelight, no matter the cost. When the girls in her friendship group found her too domineering and pulled away, Maxine began picking on the same girls she'd once hoped to befriend.

From spreading untrue stories to stealing some of their prized stationery, she made life difficult for the girls whom she felt had betrayed her. Maxine struggled to realise that friends weren't people she could boss around and try to control so she'd feel accepted. She came across as innocent and sweet in front of teachers and coaches but had a dark and unkind side that revealed itself when she was with her peers. Her trying to gain popularity by bringing others down wasn't winning her any real friendships. She'd become the talk of the playground for all the wrong reasons.

My first task with Maxine was to help her understand that respect from peers is something to be earned, not demanded. Then we began Maxine's journey to rebuilding her friends' trust. Along the way, it was important for her to understand how her behaviour was impacting not only others, but her as well. Together, we worked out what was driving her bullying behaviour, which allowed her to see just how low her self-esteem was. Eventually, she was able to feel more secure in herself, which helped make it easier for her to make friends.

No one wants to hear that their child is a bully. When this call comes, many parents are surprised, ashamed or even outraged. In these situations, it's important to take action right away – not only to help your daughter own up to her mistakes and make repairs but also to understand her reasoning behind this behaviour.

There are many reasons why children bully others.[56] Sometimes it's because they're being bullied and are looking for a way to feel in control of a situation for once. Other times, children (like Maxine) bully to hide their insecurities, or because they think it will help make them more popular at school. Then there are children who have difficulty regulating their emotions or expressing them in a healthy way.[57]

Understanding your daughter's motivations for bullying will go a long way towards helping remedy the situation. It may also open a window into her social life, if you're able to approach the situation without shame or judgement. Keep your tone light and listen as much as possible. The angrier you are, the more likely it is that your daughter will become withdrawn or shut down completely.

Here are some ways to take action if your daughter is accused of bullying.

1. Address the problem immediately. Approach the conversation with an open mind and ask her to tell the story from her point of view. Don't assign blame until you've heard both sides of the story.

2. Express to her how the friend or peer she bullied may be feeling right now. While it's important to listen to her feelings, it's also important that she understands how her behaviour has impacted others.

3. Ask her to explain the reasoning behind her behaviour. As we've discussed, children bully for many different reasons, including wanting to fit in or because they're being bullied themselves.

4. Help her brainstorm actions that she can take next time a similar situation comes up.

It might be helpful to use these phrases during your conversation:

- 'I love you very much, but bullying is unacceptable and this behaviour will have to change.'

- 'What were you feeling when you hurt your friend? Can you think of a better way to express those feelings next time?'

- 'Are you able to see how your behaviour hurt your friend?'

- 'How can I help you feel better?'

- 'What can you do to help make your friend feel better?'

Key points to land on

Conscious approaches to speaking and listening to girls will help foster greater levels of empathy. With empathy skills, girls will have more successful and healthier relationships with themselves and others. Having the ability to rethink situations and see them from different perspectives gives our girls a stronger foundation from which to build their education.

Discussing and sharing what healthy friendships should look like with tween girls is essential for them to learn the difference between a strong and giving friendship and one that is built on competition, control and mistrust. The more we can support our girls' growth in these critical areas, the better they'll fare making friends on their own.

If we encourage our girls to consistently ask themselves, 'How do I want to show up as a friend today?' they'll display increased empathy for others and learn to be upstanding citizens and role models for others in the process.

FOUR
Emotional Intelligence

Before taking off

Being in touch with the countless emotions that girls are experiencing at this stage and being able to understand how to accept and name them will help them build healthier and more meaningful relationships, so emotional intelligence is the crucial third step of the five-step methodology.

The term 'emotional intelligence' was coined by psychologists nearly thirty years ago, but it's recently become quite a buzzword. As research progresses, we've come to realise the value of emotional intelligence and how individuals with more of this quality are in a better position to make decisions.[58]

Psychology professor John D. Mayer originally defined emotional intelligence as 'the ability to accurately perceive your own and others' emotions; to understand the signals that emotions send about relationships; and to manage your own and others' emotions'.[59] Most girls aren't actively taught the social and emotional language that allows them to be aware of their feelings. On the contrary, we've been trained to mask our feelings. If we aren't able to recognise and understand the causes or consequences of our emotions, we tend to create barriers and can lose the ability to regulate ourselves so that our emotions don't overpower our actions. Our emotions are often in control, even if we aim to supress them. It's in our nature to first gather data based on our emotions and then data to support our emotions. Girls in early adolescence are pros at this.

IQ versus EQ

Having both a high intelligence quotient (IQ) and a high emotional quotient (EQ) is, of course, the ultimate aim. A balance of these two qualities sets us up for positive results and enables personal growth. Let's look at each separately first.

IQ usually refers to intellectual ability. Some of the most common elements of IQ include the ability to:

• Use logic to solve problems

- Plan

- Strategise

- Understand abstract ideas

- Learn and adapt to change

- Grasp and use language

It's not uncommon for a girl's self-esteem to plummet if she feels she's not smart enough. This idea can seep into their internal dialogue at a young age. Girls then, more often than not, end up expending their energy trying to stand out in other ways, such as through their looks or social standing. Many girls who exert their energy in this way are simply trying to fill a deep-seated insecurity about not being 'smart' enough, especially in some of the more competitive schools where test results determine your rank. Currently, most schools emphasise exam results and assessments as measures of aptitude and intelligence. Many girls begin to take entrance tests in preschool and then must pass other knowledge-based hurdles. If the student is rejected from school at a young age, what begins to form in the girl's mind is an idea of their academic abilities based on something external.

EQ generally refers to the ability to sense emotions in ourselves and others. It also refers to how that awareness is used to guide behaviour. In general, those with a high EQ, may find it easier to:

- Identify emotions in themselves and others[60]

- Empathise with other people

- Adapt their feelings and behaviours to different situations

- Withstand temptation and delay gratification

- Resolve conflicts[61]

- Communicate effectively[62]

Many EQ tests rank a person's abilities in self-awareness, self-regulation, motivation and social skills. Developing both IQ and EQ sets our girls up for success, as each quotient enhances different areas of the brain.

Simply put, when it comes to both IQ and EQ, what's important isn't how much we know but how much we want to learn. Instilling curiosity in our girls about ideas and people leads to exploration and meaningful connections. We can teach our girls to have greater EQ. With an improved EQ, they can respond to situations in a balanced and measured way.

In an important article published in the *Harvard Business Review* in 1998, Rutgers psychologist Daniel Goleman suggests that 'without EQ, a person can have the best training in the world, an incisive, analytical mind, and an endless supply of smart ideas, but he still won't make a great leader'.[63] People with a high EQ are known to be better at challenging the status quo by speaking up with ideas and suggestions for bettering the world we live in or the places we work.

As discussed, it's worth thinking about what kind of leaders we hope our girls to grow up to be. Do we envision a world where girls are encouraged to be 'emotion scientists'[64] – people who can ask good questions to understand emotions – or leaders who have intellectual capacity without the ability to relate to others on a human level? Goleman found through his work that 'the most effective leaders are all alike in one crucial way: they all have a high degree of emotional intelligence'.[65] Oprah Winfrey is an excellent example of this. She demonstrates remarkable skill in reading the emotions of not just her interview subjects, but also her audience, and through her foundation, she puts her empathy to work and sparks emotions that move others to action.

It's not that IQ and technical skills are redundant. Of course they matter – but there's a limit to how far they can take us.

Girls and their emotions

As we've discussed, adolescence is a time of significant development inside the teenage brain. Puberty is associated with many types of changes, ranging from physical to hormonal, all of which influence our girls' emotions. All these changes coalescing at once make puberty a highly confusing time in a girl's life and can contribute to her inability to feel in control.

The main changes at this time stem from our girls' brain development. Unused connections in the thinking and processing part of their brains (called the grey matter) are 'pruned' away. Scientists call this the 'synaptic pruning process'.[66] At the same time, other connections are strengthened. This is the brain's way of becoming more efficient. It's analogous to the common phrase 'use it or lose it'.

This pruning process begins at the back of the brain. The front part of the brain, the prefrontal cortex, is remodelled last. The prefrontal cortex is the decision-making part of the brain, responsible for your child's ability to plan, think about the consequences of their actions, solve problems and control impulses. Changes in this part of the brain continue well into early adulthood. As individuals reach their late twenties, this pruning process begins to taper off.[67]

Since the prefrontal cortex is still developing, girls in early adolescence rely on a part of the brain called the amygdala to make decisions and solve problems more than adults do.[68] The amygdala is associated with emotions, impulses, aggression and instinctive behaviour. This reliance on the amygdala can help explain some of the increased emotional dysregulation in girls of early adolescence.[69] There have been many studies conducted which speak to the intensity of the emotions our girls' experience during this time.[70] During its development, the amygdala is also more vulnerable to stress than the fully developed adult brain.[71]

Occasionally, your daughter's behaviour may seem quite mature. Other times, she may behave in illogical, impulsive ways. This can be frustrating for parents and caregivers. Learning more about the back-to-front development of the brain can help shed light on these shifts and changes.

Our girls' brains are working hard. They're still under construction, and the rapid and sometimes frequent shifts in behaviour can catch parents off guard. It can be difficult for parents and carers to keep tabs on where their daughter might be from one day or even one minute to the next. Despite their Oscar-worthy dramatic performances, our girls are generally not trying to be highly emotional, sensitive or moody on purpose.

I encourage both daughters and their parents to follow these three steps when they stumble into an emotional situation:

1. Understand the emotion

2. Name the emotion

3. Feel the emotion

The more that parents and carers are able to under-stand and define their own emotions, differentiating between frustration, anger, rage and jealousy, for example, the easier it will be for our daughters to accept their emotions without becoming defensive. Nothing is more frustrating than someone assuming that they know what we're feeling. For developing girls, this feeling can be particularly acute. It often leads to phrases many of us have heard before, such as:

- 'You don't know what I'm feeling!'
- 'You just don't get it, and you never will!'
- 'You don't understand how hard it is for me!'

Parents naturally want to rebut these unfair assertions because of course they were young once and have likely had similar experiences. Unfortunately, the last thing your daughter wants from you is that level of relatability. They're desperately seeking ways to cre-ate their own identities away from you, and even well-meaning attempts to disprove these assertions rarely go well.

If we teach them to lean into and name the emotions that they're experiencing, it will be easier for them to understand and accept these feelings, no matter how irrational they may seem to an adult. For our girls, the emotions they're experiencing are valid and important.

Examples of unhelpful phrases to say to your teen or tween daughter include:

- **'What were you thinking?'** Chances are, they weren't. They're more impulsive than rational at this stage of growth.

- **'I'm going to throw your phone into the bin!'** Setting boundaries will serve you both better than empty threats.

- **'Because I said so!'** Explaining your rationale will earn you more respect.

- **'Why are you so selfish?'** Self-absorption is an inherent part of their current developmental stage. They can't help it, but you can change your behaviour to model compassion and empathy.

- **'Stop being so moody!'** It's not her – it's the surge of hormones that make her weep one minute and laugh hysterically the next. This stage will pass, but pointing out her moodiness will likely only irritate and inflame her frustrations further.

Our girls need to know that their parents aren't there to judge their emotions but instead are there to help them feel secure and safe. If you feel that your daughter is overreacting, the best time to address it isn't when her emotions are running high. Instead, postpone that conversation until her equilibrium has returned. At this time in a girl's development, being there as her coach or consultant is more important than trying to alter, control or influence her moods or actions.

Here are some examples of phrases they need us to reiterate in times of emotional distress or dysregulation:

- 'I'm already proud of you.'
- 'You matter so much to me/us.'
- 'I enjoy spending time with you.'
- 'I believe you can.'
- 'I love everything about you that makes you *you*!'
- 'I admire how hard you worked on that.'

Why it's crucial to teach EQ to young students

EQ should be viewed as a critical skill for young people to learn. With emotional intelligence, girls can better inspire and motivate others and create more meaningful bonds with their peers and families. EQ isn't only significant in creating a productive and positive learning environment – it's also an important part of self-development. Girls with a high EQ aren't as reactionary and are generally more compassionate and open-minded, and according to researchers in the field, teaching our girls to manage emotions can result in less bullying and greater cooperation.[72]

As a result of the focus on this skill in recent years, emotional intelligence is beginning to be more widely taught in secondary schools, business schools and medical schools. However, the importance of teaching it in primary and middle schools hasn't yet been recognised enough. It's particularly pertinent during the pre-adolescent stage of development, where emotions are at their most heightened and growing pains are at their peak.

Emotional intelligence isn't necessarily an intuitive skill. Resources and training are essential for parents and teachers alike. Most of us, educators included, are neither in touch with our emotions nor adequately equipped with the necessary tools to regulate them. In fact, we humans tend to be reactionary creatures who think that dealing with everything around us is the best way forward when trying to solve a problem. It's actually much more important for us to teach our girls not to worry about the noise around them but to look at how they might be able to identify, control and react to the emotions they're feeling.

Especially in times of distress, young girls tend to react in ways that they believe they need to in response to how they will be perceived by their peers. It's better for them to understand that they cannot control what is happening around them but that they *can* work on looking inwards to listen to their emotions and control their responses.

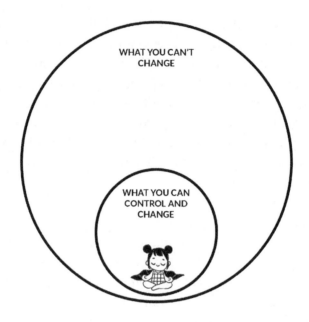

In her research, Brené Brown found that when she asked people to write down emotions they could recognise in themselves and others, the average number of emotions each participant listed was three. Most commonly, her subjects identified the emotions bad, sad and glad.[73] This is a shocking demonstration of the primitive level of understanding most of us have regarding our emotions.

The Yale Center for Emotional Intelligence is an institution that's delving deeper into questions surrounding emotional intelligence. Founding director Marc Brackett runs a social-emotional training programme called RULER, which to date has taught educators and students in more than 2,000 American schools what it means to understand and manage their emotions.[74]

The more educated students and adults are about the complexities of emotions, the better we can regulate our emotional state and have better wellness all around. Brackett is actively working with school districts to implement new curricula around emotional literacy within the middle school years.[75] Hopefully, school boards and educators in other cities and countries will use this as inspiration.

Brackett defines feelings as 'a core experience'. Emotions, on the other hand, are 'more granular, more specific'. Emotions often result from differing root causes. He explains, 'Anger is about injustice, but disappointment is about unmet expectations.'[76]

According to Wharton psychologist and professor Adam Grant, 'a core skill of emotional intelligence is treating your feelings as a rough draft. Like art, emotions are works in progress. It rarely serves you well to frame your first sketch. As you gain perspective, you can revise what you feel. Sometimes you even start over from scratch.'[77]

Research has proven that most individuals aren't able to identify the cause of their emotions and how to regulate them. In fact, most young teens are on autopilot and tend to suppress their emotions rather than deal with them. They aren't aware that repressing them doesn't make them vanish. Instead, unprocessed emotions linger and evolve, obstructing vital aspects of their growth.[78]

Emotional intelligence should be touted by leaders, policymakers and educators as one of the solutions to a wide range of social issues. It's also critical to helping raise our youth to be well-balanced individuals. We can help our girls cultivate EQ at home through practices such as mindfulness and journaling.

The importance of journaling and mindfulness

One of the challenges of working with girls in their pre-teen, tween and teenage years is their outward focus. At this age, social pressures are high, and it's easy for girls to get caught up in a cycle of peer pressure and beliefs espoused by people in their friend group. With increased reliance on devices and more time spent in school and activities, it can be a real struggle for girls to take the time to listen to their thoughts and engage in critical self-reflection. This lack of awareness can lead to an ongoing struggle with emotional intelligence.

Journaling

To encourage greater self-reflection and improve emotional intelligence, many parents have started encouraging their daughters to journal. Journaling is a fantastic habit for our girls to start, especially as they enter their tween or teenage years.

When a person puts their thoughts down on paper, they naturally begin to process them. As well, once a girl has been journaling for a while, she can look back on her writing and begin to identify patterns. Maybe she felt stronger emotions while menstruating, or during certain seasons. Identifying and understanding these patterns can be helpful.

Journaling can also have a meaningful impact on a student's academic performance. Any type of writing, even journaling, improves overall language usage, spelling, grammar and syntax.[79] When they use journaling to think through problems and propose solutions, our girls can also become more adept problem solvers.

Getting your child involved in journaling isn't as simple as providing a notebook and asking them to start writing. It might require some effort on your part to get the process going. Here are some ways you can help them start.

Help her set a goal. We're much more likely to stick to a habit when we set a concrete goal. For your daughter, this could be anything from 'I want to journal for five minutes every day' to 'I will write ten pages every week'. Help her set a goal that is both helpful and meaningful for her.

Discover a method or material that she enjoys. A girl may be more motivated to write if she likes the journal she's using, for example. If she prefers to type out her thoughts, help her find an app, such as Day One,[80] or suggest a dedicated password-protected Word document.

Set aside dedicated journaling time. Habits are much easier to maintain when they're consistent. Carving out and setting aside a little time to journal every day will strengthen the habit. In addition, she can tie it to an action. For example, 'As soon as I walk into the classroom, or before I go to bed, I'll sit at my desk and journal for five minutes.' Ensure the routine is simple and easy to follow.

Make it as easy as possible to do. Encourage her to keep her journal and writing implements in an easily accessible place. If she must search for her journal, go to another place to find a pen, then settle into a third place to write, she can quickly become discouraged from her new habit.

It's important to remember not to apply parameters. Parents and carers should resist the urge to tell girls what to write. Instead, a girl's own feelings and needs should dictate the terms of her journaling habit. If your daughter isn't a fan of journaling, that's fine too.

There are many other ways to help her bring EQ into her daily life.

Mindfulness

'Mindfulness' is a word that's said so often that it can be hard to understand what it is, exactly. Mindfulness is simply the innate human ability to be fully present in any moment. It's much trickier than it might seem. Many of us go through entire days without focusing on the present. Whether we're dwelling on something that happened yesterday or anxiously anticipating the future, it's easy to get caught up in a cycle of feelings and emotions that take us away from the here and now.

There are many ways that mindfulness can improve our day-to-day lives. One of the first things that people notice after starting a mindfulness practice is an improvement regarding ongoing anxious or depressive thoughts.[81]

Other studies have found that mindfulness helps to reduce stress and can even boost our working memory and focus,[82] making it easier to concentrate on complex tasks such as tests or homework. Some people have also found that practising mindfulness helps them be less emotionally distressed when faced with hardship or trauma.

BEDTIME BLUES

A natural worrier, Laura was having trouble falling asleep. Her mum suspected she was just a bit wired and out of sync due to the various pandemic lockdowns. Laura insisted that she had no particular worries or thoughts going round her head except for one – she was worried she wasn't getting enough sleep.

When Laura's mum wrote to me about these concerns, I thought about the best way to reset things for Laura's mind before bedtime. In our discussions, Laura shared with me that she had some bad dreams that kept waking her up. I thought that the fear and anticipation of these dreams might be keeping Laura up at night.

We tried the following exercise.

Right before she went to bed, she 'dumped her brain' onto a piece of paper by drawing out everything that she might be thinking about – essentially, she emptied her mind by putting it on paper. After she finished her doodle, she folded it and placed it into a pot, which she then put on a high shelf outside her room. This demonstrated to her that she could physically put away her worries. The physical separation of her thoughts from her brain helped her relax. She followed this with some deep breathing, the 'Buddha belly breathwork', as I refer to it. Gratefully, Laura began to relax and sleep more soundly.

Key points to land on

As Grant poignantly explains, a mark of EQ is 'treating unpleasant feelings not as unwelcome intrusions but as teachable moments'.[83]

Recent research shows that these skills can improve academic performance and graduation rates, as well as student health and well-being.[84] Building up our girls to be aware of and in touch with their emotions will also enable them to express greater care and understanding for others.

To help your daughter identify her feelings, encourage her to try the following:

• Grab a pen and list all the worries you might have at a given moment

• Don't judge whether or not your thoughts are valid

• Voice your thoughts as well as writing them down – talk them through with an adult or friend

• Identify any physical symptoms being experienced (headache or stomach ache, nervous shaking or tapping, clenching of jaw or fists)

• Draw it out

It's more important than ever to understand what EQ is and how it can help both adults and children better understand themselves, their surroundings and each other. After all, as inspired by the words of Helen Keller, 'the best and most beautiful things in the world cannot be seen nor even touched, but just felt in the heart', then surely emotional intelligence is something worth investing in.[85]

FIVE
Resilience

Before taking off

Setbacks are a part of life. Rather than shielding our girls from these types of situations, we must instead teach them how to get back up after a fall and use it as a learning opportunity.

Understanding how to prepare ourselves for tough situations both mentally and physically is a key tool in building resilience. This crucial skill will help our girls learn to accept failures and alter their preconceived notions of perfection.

This chapter will offer suggestions on how to raise girls with the ability to navigate the tumultuous period of their teen years and provide them with the tools to succeed into adulthood.

Cultivating resilience

What is resilience? To most, it's the ability to bounce back. It's fighting back after an unexpected hit. Resilience means facing hardship without losing your spirit and being courageous enough to take on change, especially unexpected change, while still allowing yourself to be vulnerable. After all, what is vulnerability if not courage?

However you define resilience, it's an incredible quality sought out by adults and youth alike. Many parents wish to see this attribute in their children, educators in their students, employers in their employees and coaches in their players.

Popular culture has made many believe that positive thinking alone is all we need to change and adapt to tough circumstances. When designing the Elevate.RA mentorship programme, I thought about resilience often. *Is it innate,* I wondered, *or is it something that can be nurtured? Will changing our thinking patterns help?*

To gain further insight, I read the book *I Still Love You*, by well-known resilience researcher Dr Michael Ungar, a Canadian family therapist.[86] It helped me to appreciate the innate potential of all pre-teens and teens, no matter their backgrounds, to live fulfilled lives with resilience – as long as they're given the right support.

With thoughtful prose and plenty of research-based content, Dr Ungar explains that the ability to thrive in hard situations isn't innate. Instead, we need people and opportunities that will give us what we need to thrive. The idea of innate resilience is a myth that allows us to avoid the truth.

According to his theory, children are like the seeds of a sunflower. If planted in fertile ground protected from irritants, they can grow despite setbacks. Cared for with love and attention, they can grow tall and sturdy, their faces pointed towards the bright light of a supportive, nurturing parent, teacher or friend.

A problem-free life isn't an interesting one, nor is it attainable. Being able to navigate obstacles despite the emotional and physical scars we carry is a sign of resilience. According to Dr Ungar, children who flourish in a complex, ever-changing world of pressures need the following nine things:

1. Structure

2. Consequences

3. Parent–child connections

4. Lots and lots of relationships

5. A powerful identity

6. A sense of control

7. A sense of belonging, spirituality and life purpose

8. Rights and responsibilities

9. Safety and support

The truth is that not all families can nurture resilience. This is due to myriad reasons, including the fact that society is neither fair nor just. When children cannot get what they need from their families, then educators, mentors and society at large must take greater responsibility when it comes to providing the essential ingredients to instil resilience in our children.

We need to build interconnected communities (more in Chapter Six) and work as teams to build our girls up. A great way to create community connections is for carers to encourage girls to seek support in the form of mentorship or guidance. This kind of support will help equip our girls with the skills they require to continue shining brightly even in the darkest of days.

Dr Ungar's principles are clear and enlightening, yet they're a tough ask. All the more reason for us to take a closer look at our own habits and behaviours when faced with adversity, so that we don't let the next generation down. Even the smallest steps towards some internal reflection to raise awareness from adults on their own relationship with handling setback or challenge can have a transformative effect on our young people.

Strength is often associated with resilience, but it comes in many forms. For girls to be strong, they must take care of both their physical and mental health. Their ability to be resilient relies on their physical, mental and emotional well-being. They must be functioning at an optimal level to meet the countless challenges of adolescence. In the early adolescent phase, the most crucial ways to strengthen physical and mental health are getting enough exercise and fresh air, getting enough sleep and maintaining a healthy diet. These things will also aid in her emotional development.

T(w)eens and exercise

Physical exercise strengthens our mental faculties both directly and indirectly. Exercise induces positive physical changes, such as a reduction in inflammation and insulin resistance.[87] Exercise also acts directly on the brain itself – studies have shown that the areas of the brain that control thinking and memory are almost always larger in individuals who exercise regularly.[88] This is true in our youth and remains the case throughout our life, as studies on both middle-aged and elderly adults have confirmed.[89]

It can also affect our mood. Exercise has been shown to increase the production of various growth-oriented chemicals throughout our bodies. One of these is BDNF (brain derived neurotrophic factor), which plays a critical role in the development and growth of the brain. A lack of BDNF is associated with increased depression and even suicidality.[90]

T(w)eens and sleep

As our girls grow up, they'll naturally seek to set their own schedule and exercise control over their daily habits. Parents tend to worry most about their daughters' well-being in regards to their sleep and diet. Helping our girls set good habits in these areas will improve their resilience.

Given that the transition to adulthood brings important physical and psychological changes that affect emotions, personality, social and family life, and academics, sleep is essential during this time. The brain and body are working behind the scenes to allow teens to be at their best. Unfortunately, research indicates that many teens get far less sleep than they need.[91]

The National Sleep Foundation and the American Academy of Sleep Medicine agree that teens need between eight and ten hours of sleep per night. This helps facilitate healthy growth and development.[92]

Teens who are active, exercise regularly or have ongoing health issues may need more sleep. Not getting enough sleep has been linked to poor mental health, since we process a lot of the day's emotional information during REM sleep.[93]

Here are a few easy tips to help with better sleep:

- Turn off all screens and electronics sixty minutes before bed.
- Buy an alarm clock, so there's no need to have devices in the bedroom overnight.
- Once in bed, and just before going to sleep, spend some time doing the following:
  - Read a chapter of your favourite novel.
  - Listen to a relaxing playlist.
  - Take a long, hot shower or bath.
  - Try some deep breathing or a mindfulness activity.
- If you need a short nap during the day, take one, but never after 3pm.
- Use the bed only for sleeping. Try to avoid using it for homework, socialising or hobbies.
- Exercise during the day.
- Try to wake up at the same time every day.

Most of our learning occurs in the first two or three years of life. We build on this foundation as we grow, and we hit another major formative period in the tween and teenage years. Getting the recommended amount of sleep can help teens maintain their physical health, emotional well-being and, consequently, their school performance. During both periods of growth, sleep is essential. It aids in the following:

- Maintaining a healthy body

- Keeping the immune system working well

- Maintaining good social, emotional and mental health

- Boosting energy levels

- Learning

- Concentration

- Improving long-term memory

Just as your devices require recharging, so does your brain. A good night's sleep will help teens and tweens keep up a positive outlook and bravely face the challenges of each day. Our youth must learn how to organise and understand their schedules so they can accomplish everything they need to do in a day without sacrificing their sleep. If our daughters can tire themselves out naturally with physical activities during the day, they'll likely sleep better at night.

It's also important for both parents and teens to understand that their natural body clock will change.

Starting around the age of twelve, melatonin production in our body changes. Melatonin is a hormone made in the body to regulate night and day cycles or sleep-wake cycles.[94] Darkness triggers the body to make more melatonin, which signals the body to sleep, and light decreases melatonin production and signals the body to be awake.

The production of melatonin in early adolescence is delayed from a natural release at around 8pm to a much later time of 11pm. It will continue to be released until after sunrise, making it challenging to get up in the morning for many teens and tweens.[95]

T(w)eens and diet

We've already discussed the impact that eating disorders can have on girls. It is important to be mindful about the messages being presented to girls around diet and what healthy diets look like. You don't have to study nutrition to know that the foods we eat influence our physical well-being, but science is now coming to a greater understanding regarding the links between nutrient intake and mental health. More and more connections are being discovered every day.

In studies on the diets of individuals with depression, the most common nutrient deficiencies researchers found were omega-3 fatty acids, vitamin B (folate) and magnesium. Demographic research has determined that populations that eat a lot of fish tend to have lower rates of mental disorders, likely in part because of their elevated levels of omega-3 fatty acids.[96]

Some simple ways to help your daughter improve her diet, which in turn will have a positive effect on her mental health, include the following:

- Cutting down on foods that are high in sugar

- Reducing white carbohydrate intake

- Making sure every meal includes both protein and healthy fat

- Supplementing her diet with omega-3, zinc, folate or magnesium, if recommended by a doctor

Flexibility and plan B

The COVID-19 pandemic brought to light how easily the best-laid plans can be disrupted by forces out of our control. Many of us have learned that plan A may not go as expected.

It's my hope that these lessons in flexibility and creative thinking, as witnessed in the ways home-schooling was delivered, for example, will encourage educators and parents to prioritise the value of teaching young people about resilience. We simply cannot assume that they'll one day get it without laying the groundwork first.

The realisation that sudden unknowns can cascade into our daily lives and cause mass disruption has been observed worldwide. Adapting to these changes has led many to refer to the days ahead as the 'new normal'. The importance of having a plan B, or at least acknowledging that our plan A may not work, is more apparent than ever before. When teaching resilience, it's vital to reiterate that there can always be a plan B, or a plan C, for that matter. Often, in hindsight, those with wisdom and experience share that plan B led to a better outcome than hoped for with plan A. This isn't always easy to see at first, yet perseverance in not giving up on a goal when plan A does not work can help our girls become more resilient in meaningful ways.

The ability to view setbacks or roadblocks as an opportunity to build skills in innovation and creative thinking is an asset. Framing our conversations around resilience while offering relatable examples can help prepare our girls to be flexible.

TOUGH TIMES IN TWEEN YEARS

Amelie is eleven years old and was diagnosed with dyslexia early in childhood. She often found certain elements of learning a challenge. Despite her being a bright and enthusiastic student, the schools she attended often weren't equipped to support her. As a result, she became accustomed to having to change schools.

At a specialist school, she studied diligently and learned many new ways to navigate mainstream school expectations. She was just about to head back into a mainstream school, having jumped through several hurdles, including a rigorous entrance test, when her plans changed.

The COVID-19 pandemic hit. Her parents were facing great economic strain due to their family income being dependent on the restaurant and entertainment sectors. This strain took a major toll on her parents, who decided to separate. Amelie, along with her brother and mother, moved out of the family home. Her father started a new job in a new country, making visits challenging, especially during a global pandemic.

Adding to these enormous changes was the fact that Amelie's new school announced that it would be pivoting to remote learning. Isolated and confronted with loss and change, Amelie became distraught. In our work together, we cultivated strategies that enabled her to take control of her emotions while accepting the changes that were still unfolding around her.

It was essential for us to consider the flexibility of an elastic brain and strategies to overcome the sadness of initial plans not working out. Working with Amelie was refreshing, and it was such a joy to watch her demonstrate resilience as she took on her new reality. Soon, she was making an effort to make new friends virtually, and she learned to accept that her parents were healthier and happier when not married to each other.

Failure

Fear of failure

A girl's desire to try something new or go after a dream is often dampened by her fear of failure. We need to normalise failure. Instead of being ashamed of it, we must look at it as something that can connect us all. It's something that every girl, no matter her background, class or colour, has encountered or will encounter. Being afraid of failure won't help us. Instead, we must do what children's author Katherine Rundell mentioned in a recent conversation on The Elevate Podcast: 'shake hands with fear.'[97] If we encourage our girls to accept that fear is universally felt, it may help them feel less alone and will hopefully reduce the anxiety they feel around failure.

'I'm a failure' is a common phrase uttered by young girls – unsurprisingly so, as they continually put themselves under societal, parental and academic pressure to perform. They're given subliminal and, often, overt messages to do better and be better, and they're likely holding themselves up to the curated standards of perfection seen on social media and TV. They're led to believe they aren't clever enough, sociable enough, thin enough, popular enough or athletic enough by the unrealistic standards they witness all around them. Instead of allowing them to say 'I'm a failure', we should encourage our girls to say 'that was a failed attempt'.

This is only the first step in teaching our girls to rethink failure. Failure has historically and commonly been viewed as the opposite of success. In reality, it's a critical part of success. Most successful individuals will tell you that success isn't linear. There are dips and plateaus on the journey. We should endeavour to help our girls see dips or plateaus as periods of rest that will aid their ability to tackle new things. Dismantling these notions around failure can help girls understand that failing isn't a wound as huge as they imagine.

YOUR GOALS

FAILING ONCE   FAILING AGAIN AND AGAIN

This fear of failure isn't something all girls are born with. Many are inherently cautious, but you may remember your little darlings taking risks when they were younger, such as jumping from high monkey bars, speeding down a hill on their bike or speaking their mind about the taste of a meal at a friend's house.

Somewhere during their development, though, many girls begin to seek external validation and doubt themselves. To combat this, we must actively fight against the stigmatisation of failure and help them accept or even celebrate failure as an opportunity for growth. As soon as they let their fear go, they'll begin to score wins, opening up so many new possibilities.

Here are some examples of positive things we can say to an anxious tween or teen:

- 'It's OK to feel nervous. I do too sometimes.'
- 'Let's draw the fear. How big is it?'
- 'Let's talk back to this fear.'
- 'I'm here for you.'
- 'Let's sit together until this fearful thought passes.'

Addressing fear around failure may be what prevents our girls from giving up before they start trying. As a teacher, I saw girls who were so paralysed by the fear of failure that they were unwilling to try something new. Their imagined failure motivated them to claim helplessness, which was astonishing and demoralising to witness.

Learned helplessness

Learned helplessness is the outcome of believing that our behaviour has no influence on consequences or events. This often manifests as students setting themselves up to fail before they even try. Ultimately, it can lead to students believing that they're not capable of overcoming the difficulties they face.

This is more prevalent in girls than boys. Increasingly, I've seen girls declare that they're unable to take on a challenge or work out a problem for themselves before they've put in any honest effort. The underlying problem is that their lack of effort causes failure, reinforcing their negative beliefs about themselves. Although learned helplessness can develop in students who don't fail that often, children who repeatedly fail are at much greater risk of developing it.

The fact that girls are more vulnerable to learned helplessness can be attributed to a few different causes, including perfectionism. Jenna Palumbo, a mental health therapist, affirms that adolescent girls are particularly susceptible to perfectionism. 'Stereotypically, girls are given so much more praise when they're polite, attentive, people-pleasing and easy to work with,' she says.[98]

Our society has tended to praise boys for being tough and girls for their appearance and good behaviour. In a school setting, this can lead girls to avoid behaviours that may draw attention to their perceived flaws. The illusion of perfection can be so compelling that the risk of making errors is too distressing for them to even attempt the task. Many girls work themselves into a panic about being publicly shamed or called out on a mistake in front of their peers, which can override any intrinsic motivation to take such risks.

When a girl is quite young, this perfectionism may be seen as an asset, making school a breeze. When she enters middle school, though, topics become more challenging and students are required to ask questions and make mistakes in order to learn the concepts. This may be a struggle for perfectionists. In these challenging situations, many girls adjust their behaviour to seek acceptance.

A reliance on others who are readily available to 'help' girls solve problems may make the issue worse. Many parents who can afford external support hire tutors, for example, for their daughters who are struggling to keep up with schoolwork. This may make some children believe that they don't have the resources or abilities to tackle their work alone. They may wait for a friend to pass on the solutions or claim ignorance in class and wait for teachers to spell out explanations for them. In these scenarios, the child has embraced the narrative that they're helpless, so they don't try to alter their reality even though change is possible.

Carol Dweck and her associates have studied learned helplessness, and their findings have been published by the American Psychological Association. In their work, they found that girls, rather than boys, showed greater evidence of learned helplessness in achievement situations. Girls often attributed their failures to lack of ability, rather than motivation.[99] Learned helplessness often results in passive learners who are too afraid of failure to try new things. Rather than study or work at something to improve their knowledge (which requires effort, grit and resilience), they give up on themselves before they even try because of their fear of failure.[100]

What can we do, as educators and parents, to dismantle learned helplessness? Most importantly, we should try to raise young people who are less dependent and much more self-reliant. We can help our girls build resilience by showcasing examples of how failures can lead to success. We can also model courage by displaying vulnerability – through taking risks ourselves. These two actions are key.

Teachers and parents must also be mindful of how they praise girls. They shouldn't use limiting language. Instead, they should use growth-mindset phrases, providing encouragement and offering help only if the student has had an honest try at something first. We should be rewarding effort, not results. We should be moving towards a mindset where kids are encouraged, not signed up for extra tuition every time they find a subject difficult. This can quickly become a crutch.

Showing children tough love, on occasion, may be the most important form of support. Letting kids fail and teaching them the value of getting back up on their own terms is monumental to ensuring we're setting them up for success. There's so much merit in tackling something on your own. Ultimately, we need to get students comfortable with being in discomfort.

It's also important to praise our daughters for things that really count. We often forget to praise effort in the moment and look only at what's being presented to us, which might be a result your daughter wasn't hoping for. Rewarding effort, not outcome, is crucial to their development, though. As Dweck explains, 'If we praise effort, we produce students who approach difficult tasks with the knowledge that their hard effort, not their natural gifts, can and will help them succeed.'[101]

When you reward hard work, more hard work will follow. If you reward only achievement, the hard work may stop when it becomes too difficult or once the task is completed.

Rewarding effort instils autonomy and allows girls to take ownership. It can ignite passion in them to tackle or attempt something similar or even more challenging. It can also help build intrinsic motivation. If the focus is always on the outcome, the process becomes a means to an end. Emphasising the *process* of learning opens students up to the joys of overcoming academic challenges.

The benefits of failure

When one door shuts another one opens, but we have to turn the handle to get inside and see what awaits us. If we, as adults, reflect on our own experiences, we can see that most failures offer us insight into ourselves. This is no different for young girls. They may not find it easy to accept certain truths about themselves at first, but with the right tools, it can be so freeing. Failure brings with it lessons that cannot be learned in a classroom, over the dinner table or through films, TV or music. Failure is a rite of passage for our girls to experience.

Through failure, we can begin to truly appreciate the value of hard work, determination and perseverance. The pride in the energy poured into something takes precedence over everything else, and the character-building that comes along with it fosters a deeper appreciation for the achievements that ultimately come.

Failing at something doesn't make us a failure. This is an important message we need to convey to our girls. We must acknowledge failure as a fact of life. If we can engrain this notion and start to find the benefits of failure, we'll have a chance at normalising this taboo concept.

Sharing our failures and modelling perspective with a sense of humour can reassure girls that if adults have made errors and survived, they surely can as well. Embracing failure head-on and learning ways to manage their negative self-talk can help our girls soar. Instead of worrying about falling, they'll begin to see how high they can fly. For them to reach these heights, they do require support, in the form of both encouragement and feedback. Few girls can do this all on their own. To get the full benefits of learning how to fail, a girl needs a strong network of people who can remind her of her goals and how she can adapt her approach if she stumbles. Redefining failure for girls is a way to fill them with hope. They don't always have to be the best. They must *try* their best and let the rest take care of itself.

JK ROWLING

A great example of this approach to success is JK Rowling, the author of the best-selling Harry Potter series. She admits that if she'd succeeded at anything else in life, she would never have found the determination to succeed in the one arena where she believed she truly belonged. Her original manuscripts were rejected time and again, and along the way she encountered agents who told her that she'd never make any money from her stories. Additionally, her parents believed that she should have taken a different career path.[102]

Her initial failures never stopped her from pursuing her dream of becoming a writer. She had many reasons to give up and take on other work, including being a struggling single mum. Instead, she took a risk and didn't succumb to her failures. In return, she achieved incredible success.

As we all know, the Harry Potter series is one of the most incredible accomplishments in publishing history. Her books have captivated the minds of millions of children and adults worldwide.

Grief and loss

Coming to terms with loss is another component of cultivating resilience in our youth. Loss is a hard fact of life, and one that can be even more devastating to someone who hasn't yet developed resilience.

Life is unpredictable. It's an ever-evolving journey that we all must come to terms with. As much as we might want to believe that life is a smooth road ending in happily ever after, this simply isn't the reality for most. Wanting this simple life is understandable. After all, why shouldn't every teen have parents who stay married and attend their graduation ceremonies, siblings who are like friends, pets who adore them and holidays that fill their heart with joyful memories? After all, this is the case in almost every traditional story written for young girls, right? We often underestimate the power of these stories and narratives that are fed to our subconscious minds.

It's important to recognise and appreciate good fortune when we have it. It's equally important to teach our children how to roll with the punches so that even when they're caught off guard, they can manage the situation. We must teach our children that change is inevitable. Good times pass, as do bad times. Learning how to adapt in order to grow through these ups and downs is key for all of us.

As our girls start mapping out their idea of a 'perfect' life – filled with great loves, dates with their crushes, holidays with their besties, spa days with their mothers, driving lessons with their dads, first summer jobs, etc – it will seem so exciting and tantalisingly close that when their perfectly planned dreams are shattered due to things out of their control, it may be difficult for them to pick up the pieces. We will all face loss of some kind at some point. Equipping our girls when they're young to cope with loss will provide them with an ability to take the inevitable harder hits and build the necessary armour they need to survive.

When cancer crept into our home unexpectedly and took our rock, our family's foundation, away from us when I was only thirteen, I struggled in more ways than I could possibly comprehend at the time. Nothing could have changed the tragic outcome, but I do think that some preparation for the loss and the new life I was about to lead could have made my teen years easier to bear.

The heartache of loss isn't something we seek out, but it exists. It's tempting to avoid these feelings of discomfort by suppressing them, bottling them up and burying them. This almost guarantees that we'll never truly understand how to work through them. Even without intending to, we often model to our girls that it's easier to gloss over feelings than to get into the weeds of dealing with hardship. We usually ask people how they're doing as a formality. We aren't looking for the truth – we just want to get on to the bigger, more important interactions of the day. At a young age, girls learn that it's best and easiest to reply with the standard 'fine'.

When we block tough emotions and refuse to sit with discomfort, we inadvertently set our girls up to face these problems over and over again at different phases in their lives. During puberty, girls will develop questions about everything from gender and sexuality to friendships and boundaries. It's important that we have these conversations with them and provide them with space to share whatever is on their mind, from curiosity to worry and fear about the changes they are experiencing. However trivial they seem to the adults around them, these are important emotions for our girls. Rather than dismissing their feelings, we must teach them ways to get mentally, emotionally and physically fit. This is all part of self-care.

As psychotherapist and grief specialist Julia Samuel explains, 'if we can accept the pain of change and learn how to adapt, we'll then have the energy and confidence to take steps that move us forward, rather than hold us back.'[103]

Times of uncertainty undoubtedly fill most humans with fear, and each of us has a unique response to change. Taking the time to work on our inner selves through honest reflection and sharing the truth of our distress and sadness as we navigate change can connect us to each other. The future seems even more unpredictable than ever. Getting through change isn't something we can do alone. We need to rely on each other and give our girls the best shot at learning ways to ride the waves as they come, remembering that 'this too shall pass'.

Samuel also points out that grief doesn't hit us in tidy phases and stages, nor is it something that we can forget and move on from. Rather, it's an individual process that has a momentum of its own.[104] Difficult times will come, but they will also go. How we address our feelings in these times can be something we model positively for our girls.

LILA'S GRIEF

Lila's dad passed away just before the Christmas holidays, shortly after he and Lila's mother decided to separate. Eleven-year-old Lila was just about to begin senior school when we started working together. Quietly confident and extremely independent, she was good at getting herself organised for school and looking after herself and the rest of her family. But coping with the unexpected loss of her father, not knowing what to say to her new friends at school, and accepting that her family was never going to look the same again were sources of great heartache.

The essential first step in our work together was my taking the time to gain Lila's trust before asking her to share her emotions around the worry she was experiencing. Next, I worked with her to highlight her strengths, including her compassion for her mother and older brother, and constantly reminded her that she needn't go through this alone. Lila matured quicker than many girls in some ways because both her parents worked long hours in her younger years. Her reliance on problem-solving also shaped her thoughts and her grieving process. Helping Lila understand that voicing her concerns, whether through a journal or talking things through with her mother, would help her work through the grief she was experiencing.

This offered her some solace, and ultimately her relationship with her mother became stronger as Lila learned to become a better communicator. After working together over the course of two months, she felt more confident about facing the changes senior school would bring and wholeheartedly believed that no new obstacle would be insurmountable after everything she'd experienced.

Key points to land on

Resilience is a powerful skill for girls to gain. Allowing adolescent girls to discover that adversities can be viewed as teaching tools is a huge part of ensuring we raise them to be strong.

When it comes to building resilience, it's important that girls:

- Know that asking for help when faced with a challenge isn't a sign of weakness

- Create a support circle of positive relationships (family, other caring adults and friends)

- Have access to health and counselling support (including for mental health and/or addiction)

- Are reminded that others believe in them and their potential

- Feel connected to school, sports and/or extracurricular communities

- Respect others' worth and value, recognising that everyone has strengths and weaknesses

- Realise that change and challenges are part of everyday life and that they can adjust to situations

- Think creatively, building an attitude which harbours a willingness to try and fail

- Keep on trying (perseverance)

- Understand that setbacks are part of the territory and failure can be a real positive

- Laugh at things, including themselves, to see situations in a different way and relieve tension

SIX
Kindness

Before taking off

Often the most undervalued trait, but one that holds great strength as an attribute, is that of kindness. The following chapter explores the final step of the five-step methodology and how to work towards creating a society that works and lives by examples of kindness. In exploring the historical beliefs around human nature, ideas behind unkindness and how girls can spread kindness, we can build communities and a world that will work together.

Kindness can mean many different things to different people. The best way to understand the meaning of kindness is to examine your life for relevant examples. If you spend a few minutes thinking about it, you'll likely be able to remember times when you showed or were shown empathy, acceptance or thoughtfulness. For many people, the most meaningful way to show kindness is to be helpful, or to do something without expecting anything in return. Being kind goes beyond being nice. Being kind can often involve a personal cost – it's not always easy to be kind. It takes work and requires care, thought and effort.

Many people experience a lack of sincerity when faced with people who are being nice. Niceness tends to be more about upholding societal norms than about acknowledging another person's unique humanity. Striving for kindness, rather than niceness, begins with the choices that we make as individuals every day.

Kindness and science

It's in our nature to learn by watching others, which is why our behaviour, especially around our children, is so important. Young folks learn kindness by observing what the adults around them do, which includes how they treat others and themselves.

For centuries, scientists and researchers have been observing and studying the evolutionary basis of kindness to quantify the development of this deeply personal quality. Studies inspired by the work of Charles Darwin have found that as our brains evolved, we developed into a kind and caring species, with an evolutionary tendency towards sympathy and kindness rather than self-preservation.[105]

It might seem strange that the biologist who is most famous for his theory on the 'survival of the fittest' is also associated with theories on the inherent goodness of human beings. It's worth reflecting on Darwin's theories on why humans have survived and thrived for so long. In his seminal work *Descent of Man*, Darwin argues that humans are 'a profoundly social and caring species', and our tendency towards altruism and sympathy are biological imperatives rather than social constructs. While our individual survival often requires us to be selfish, the continued well-being and even existence of society requires us to care about others.[106] Our ability to do this is built into our central nervous system. When we see another human being suffering, areas of our brain associated with our pain response light up, just as they would if we were the ones in pain. Our amygdala (the area of the brain associated with our biological threat response) activates as well, as a way of telling us that since the other person is suffering, there's a real possibility that we could be affected in the same way.[107]

Interconnected communities

One small kind act can cause a ripple effect that impacts an entire community. If we encourage all girls to focus on being kind, we can create a movement. We can grow from a connected community to an interconnected society and ultimately a world that works with each other not against one another. An interconnected world is one where we acknowledge our dependence on each other.

When somebody does something kind for us, we're naturally inclined to reciprocate. By its very nature, kindness has the power to cause a chain reaction. This chain reaction is a key component of creating a more interconnected world, one in which the physical and mental health of those within it is improved. One study found that people with stronger social relationships had a 50% increased likelihood of survival than those with weaker social relationships.[108] Another report found that loneliness impacts our mortality more than both cigarette smoking and obesity.[109]

An interconnected world can facilitate the creation of more inclusive networks for our girls. When we feel connected to others, we aren't scared to ask for help when we need it, and if we take the time to be kind and help others in need, they'll naturally want to help us in return.

This is a world that we want our children to grow up in. One with stronger communities and increased reliance on each other rather than one with an outsized focus on competition. Being able to collaborate with others and perform kind acts are valuable skills that will pay dividends throughout our lives.

Of course, it's one thing to understand that we're pre-disposed to kindness and another thing to live it out on a daily basis. To achieve the kind of interconnected world we'd like to see, we must help girls learn how their behaviour affects others. Adolescent girls can be impulsive, and as their parents, we must help them create greater awareness around certain behaviours, such as thinking before speaking, forgiving instead of seeking revenge, and considering long-term relation-ships instead of short-term pride. Regular reminders about kindness and empathy can be especially help-ful if we happen to witness our daughter speak or act unkindly.

False kindness

Many young people are faced with insincerity from their peers during this time of growth. When trying to fit in and work out new friendships, it's understand-able that girls can misinterpret certain behaviours.

For instance, a young teen may express an offer of support in class without any intention of follow-ing through. Many girls broadcast false kindness to gain social credibility from others, including their peers, teachers, coaches and parents. According to psychologists, there are many reasons why girls might display false kindness.[110]

Narcissism: Some people care more about accomplishing their goals than they do about other people. They'll use their social skills to influence people in service of personal gain. This is common among teenagers because of their stage of development, because they often lack the ability to weigh their personal gain against the expense of it. That is to consider the question: at what cost am I doing this for? As the different components of their brains mature with development, many are able to set greater morals around decision-making.

Control: Girls should pay attention to friends who are kind to them but judgemental, mean or cruel to others. Selective kindness can be a form of social control exercised to ensure loyalty. Many girls have a rosy view of their friends because they experience only their kindness.

Insecurity: Girls who feel insecure often jump to negative conclusions, including attributing ulterior motives to simple kindness. This can often lead to their using 'kindness' to obtain favours.

As our girls grow, we as parents and carers must help them see the difference between true kindness and false kindness. This can be hard to learn, especially as girls are in the throes of their emotions during their pre-teen and teen years. There are bound to be occasions when others let them down with false kindness. Highlight the potential causes behind these behaviours to reinforce that it isn't about them but about the underlying feelings and emotions of the person exhibiting those actions.

Celebrating differences

We've all urged our girls to feel proud of who they are. It's a common refrain in everything from pop songs to academia. The pressure that we put on girls to feel proud of who they are can sometimes be a reflection of our desire to avoid our own responsibility in embracing differences. Young girls are their own greatest critics and tend to judge themselves against a curated ideal. Its unattainability doesn't stop girls from doing everything possible to achieve it anyway.

For example, girls with learning challenges often spend much of their time overcompensating for their differences rather than addressing them directly. This is largely due to shame. They spend so much energy trying to fit in that anything that sets them apart from the crowd becomes an embarrassment and a source of shame. Our girls will never be proud of their unique characteristics until they can create belief in themselves from within.

It's important to consider where this shame and embarrassment comes from and how we as parents can make a difference. How can girls be expected to be proud of who they are if we as a society don't make a greater effort to celebrate differences? We spend more time covering up our children's differences than speaking about them openly. Even a small effort to speak about these differences plainly would create more opportunities for growth and understanding. If we all stopped trying to blend in and showed more compassion to others, perhaps this behaviour would trickle down to our girls.

Think about the last time you saw a child having a breakdown in a public place. Did you smile and show compassion? Or did you look over sternly, or even make a judgemental comment?

Criticism of parents who are just trying to cope with a difficult situation informs society's behaviours and beliefs surrounding social acceptance. Over time, parents learn that people in public places aren't com-passionate to their child's differences. It isn't long before the child has learned that their behaviours or differences are shameful.

Inevitably, these types of situations result in the child developing low self-esteem. In preadolescence, a period in development that is already turbulent, low self-esteem can lead girls to a place of great worry and angst. This correlates to poor performance and results both in and out of school. These poor results make the child feel like a failure, reaffirming their low self-worth. It's a vicious cycle.

The 'star' table

Historically, we've isolated and alienated girls with differences. Consider how schools addressed children with unique learning profiles only a generation ago. They were asked to sit together at a special table. To be charitable, in some situations, this setting apart came from a place of good intentions. I have worked with teachers who used shapes to name their groups. The table of girls with learning differences was often known as the 'star' table.

I'm sure this ironic naming of the girls with the weakest reading and spelling skills in the class wasn't intentional. Assuming that children don't notice things like this, though, is a huge error in our understanding of their intelligence. The girls at these tables know exactly why they are there, and so does every other girl in the class.

When for example, the girls are asked to work in pairs or groups, the girls from the star table are often the last to be chosen. The children's perception of the girls' skills and abilities are a direct result of the teacher's actions.

Another tactic often used in schools, which I used myself as a learning support teacher, is taking pupils out of lessons to a special classroom, where they receive extra support. This typically involves the girl being called out by name in front of the whole class. This seems perfectly acceptable to the adult, since they see the extra lesson as something positive. To the girl who's desperately trying to fit in, being singled out for extra help makes her infer that she's not good enough or smart enough as she is. This heightens her self-doubt, as well as her belief that being different makes her inferior.

To avoid this, the language used in classrooms and schools should make extra support sessions feel special – in a positive way – for everyone. They should be as normalised as a piano lesson. If we make the notion of having to leave the classrooms for extra support lessons regarded as special or to feel proud of getting help when needed, the shame around needing extra help should naturally diminish in our children. One way to encourage this change in perspective is to actively model the different ways that students view or learn new concepts. Demonstrating the positive value that diversity adds is key to ensuring children learn that differences should be celebrated, not shamed.

An example of a technique educators can adopt in classrooms is to actively illustrate the different ways a pupil might approach a sum or write a story. Doing this reinforces the crucial message that there's more than one approach to every challenge. Once the benefits of being different are highlighted in an inclusive and celebratory way, and we allow ourselves to talk openly about accepting differences, a significant change in our girls' mindset is possible. This can have a huge effect on their self-esteem, as well as their long-term success and growth.

Understanding that children with differences may require extra help or support to address their specific needs is important and vital to their development. How we deliver this support, and the language we use to address their challenges, plays a huge role in how our girls perceive their differences. Each child is unique, and a one-size-fits-all approach won't work. Taking the time to listen, understand their personalities and find out what works for them before establishing a routine for extra support can make a major difference in how they embrace their unique challenges. Ultimately, it can help them feel empowered, not embarrassed, by their learning differences.

When we celebrate differences, we create a more vibrant, supportive place for children to grow – a place where their uniqueness adds flair and value to the overall learning and social environment. Their uniqueness becomes their superpower, enabling them to hold their head high and truly feel proud of who they are. This shift needs to start with us, not our girls. If we want young girls to feel proud of who they are and not compare themselves to anyone else, we need to normalise our language and behaviour around differences – not just in schools but also in parks, playgrounds, airports and all other public spaces.

Diversity, equity and inclusion

Being a parent doesn't mean that we have it all figured out or that we've accumulated all the wisdom necessary to impart to those we care for. Our children can be our greatest teachers. They can expose things within us and help us learn more about ourselves. In each stage of their development, they have the power to change the way we think and can enable us to discover how we're wired.

When our children are adolescents, we can ponder what our own life experiences have conditioned us to think. Our daughters have unique wisdom and perspectives. They may shed light, for instance, on the way we communicate or perhaps the unconscious biases we have, allowing us to question our thoughts on important issues.

Learning and discovery is a process, and as adults, we often forget that all the beliefs we've accumulated over the years – through our own experiences, education and upbringing – aren't necessarily correct or beneficial. Things you were taught to view as true or acceptable may not be true or acceptable today.

I invite you to unlearn the things you've learned in order to grow and move on to new ideas. Lean into some of the ideologies that speak to raising girls in a more inclusive and equal society. It will take as much work from us as it will from our girls, but they're at an impressionable age, and we can fill their minds and hearts with the thoughts and ideas that will enable them to show up in the world in better ways than the generations before them.

Standing on the shoulders of the good work done by previous generations has hopefully enabled us to lead better lives than our parents led. It's our turn to do good work for our daughters. Nothing changes if nothing changes. To be good examples for our girls, we need to take ourselves through a process of interrogation and reflection. This can be hard. It requires us to face our fears, grief and even shame regarding the ideologies and prejudices that we hold or have held. It's not something we should shy away from, though. Doing the hard work around this will only ensure we're raising our girls to be part of a society that is fundamentally more inclusive. I invite parents to ask themselves the following questions:

- What biases do I hold that need to be challenged or questioned?

- How have I been conditioned to operate and where did I learn this from?

- How can I be accountable when it comes to aligning my actions with my values?

- What beliefs and narratives are preventing me from showing up fully?

- What kind of support do I need to offer to break through cycles and not repeat them?

Diversity, equity and inclusion matters

Today's youth will soon be filling the workplaces of tomorrow. The shift in mindset around inclusion for everyone with diverse backgrounds needs to begin while they're in their pivotal years of schooling. We should never stop educating ourselves, but we start forming our belief systems and values at a young age. Providing our youth with positive messages around diversity, equity and inclusion (DEI) is vital.

Aiko Bethea is the founder of RARE Coaching & Consulting, a consulting practice focused on coaching leaders and organisations to remove barriers to inclusion. In one of her many essays on the topic of DEI, she recounts a horrifying personal experience.

'I will never forget being searched at an organisation where I served as part of the leadership team – as all of my white colleagues walked past me wondering what I did wrong. The security team learned that a bag was taken. My bag looked nothing like the one reported missing, but I was the first black person seen coming from the direction where the bag was reported missing. After this, I never brought my sons to that campus again and increased my efforts to transition out of that organisation.'[111]

This account is alarming and demoralising. It reveals how unconscious bias can shape a person's life.

Multiculturalism is our global culture, and we must actively encourage others to embrace rather than 'tolerate' blended cultures. We must normalise multiculturalism for the next generation. The question 'Where are you from?' is triggering for many people. Taking time to understand why this question, which seems quite innocent on the surface, can have a deeper impact on people will increase the understanding, awareness and overall acceptance of everyone in a culture. We must ensure we're celebrating, not isolating, people.

LGBTQ concerns in the teen years

On my podcast, I had the pleasure of sharing the story of Paria Hassouri.[112] Her journey as a mother is one of the most compelling and relatable I've ever encountered. Her feeling lost when her daughter revealed her gender to be different to the one she was born with and working on ways to find herself again during her daughter's transition led her to ask important and meaningful questions of herself. She drew on insecurities from her past and worked out how she could find a way to release herself from others' expectations.

As a physician who'd looked after children for many years, she was, or at least she thought she was, well equipped to understand young people's needs. Her life and work took a turn when she realised that perhaps she wasn't as equipped as she'd thought to help her own teenager navigate the overwhelming concerns around transition.

When her daughter came out in 2017, Paria found that there weren't many examples in the media of stories of transgender people who'd come out after starting puberty without showing signs of being transgender earlier in childhood. Everything she read or saw was about kids who'd either expressed their true gender as early as age four or five or said that they were aware of it that early but didn't act on it and suppressed it. Paria realised that she was sometimes parenting from a place of fear instead of love, which hit home for me in a major way as well. Most parents can relate to having fears around how our child will be viewed by others. Will she be bullied? How will extended family and siblings interact with her? Yet, when Paria faced her fears and began sharing her daughter's true identity, she felt a massive sense of relief and support.

It takes courage to come to terms with your insecurities as a parent. It takes vulnerability to reflect on the things you felt you got wrong. Paria is a brilliant example of someone who bravely shared her regrets in her handling of her teenage daughter's transition. I have so much empathy for her. I spent years trying to 'fix' my son's autism rather than addressing the child standing in front of me. Of course, my story is different from Paria's, but like her, I wish I'd understood the importance of parenting from a place of love and acceptance earlier. This would have helped my son avoid attending inappropriate schools, and would have helped me avoid many sleepless nights filled with anxiety. Paria mentioned the word 'shame' in her moving story. Shame is something many struggle to come to terms with, but shining a light on it can free us from its heavy weight.

People-Pleasers

People-pleasing stems from our need to feel we belong. This need is normal and natural. When a young girl's fear of rejection or criticism becomes larger than her own values and needs, though, people-pleasing behaviours can be troublesome. Often, our girls worry that they won't be accepted or respected, or that they'll be seen as inadequate in some way.

Eventually, they may convince themselves to act in-authentically to feel they belong. The vicious cycle this creates never ends. You can never do enough. The more you give, the more others expect of you. This will keep happening for our girls until they're depleted of energy and begin to feel resentful of others, as they've neglected their own needs.

People-pleasing often masquerades as being kind, and certain girls are adept at taking advantage of others' vulnerabilities to get what they want. We parents must point out, in a gentle manner, that girls who end up people-pleasing are investing in the wrong things. Being accepted starts with being kind to yourself. It doesn't require putting others before you.

WORRYING WHAT OTHERS THINK ABOUT YOU

LETTING GO OF OTHERS' EXPECTATIONS

Girls who have experienced trauma or stress can be more vulnerable to feelings of rejection or inadequacy, since these feelings confirm the bias they've developed. Helping young girls deal with distress appropriately, which might include seeking professional advice, will undoubtedly aid their development in older years.

Teaching and modelling appropriate boundaries to girls will help solidify the distinction between being kind and people-pleasing. It's worthwhile to reinforce to your daughter that boundaries don't have to be understood or agreed with to be respected. Here are some examples of what people-pleasing might look like in your daughter's everyday life:

- Doing for others what they could do for themselves

- Going out of her way to accommodate people

- Not asserting herself when people are mean or disrespectful

- Remaining silent when she has a concern

- Taking the blame consistently for other people's actions

- Doing what's best for everyone except herself

Girl power in practice

Empowering our young girls helps to ensure they can grow up to be the strong leaders of tomorrow. This empowerment begins with dismantling previously held beliefs or notions about limitations. Then, we must equip them with the tools they need to feel empowered, so they can rise to limitless achievements. This is true girl power.

To help girls celebrate their power, we can encourage them to do the following:

1. Find a few female role models and learn about how they used their intelligence as well as their empathy and kindness to achieve their goals. Strong women never tear each other down. They build each other up through the superpowers of empathy and kindness.

2. Learn about different women's experiences. There are numerous ways to be a woman in the world today. By reading books or consuming media about girls or women whose lives are different from theirs, girls can learn about the incredible possibilities of womanhood. They can also learn about what has held others back from achieving their full potential.

3. Search for their own voice and make their thoughts heard. Activities such as debating or journaling, for example, can help get girls more accustomed to listening to and trusting their inner voice.

4. Take time to examine stereotypes. A great way to begin debunking these stereotypes is to ask girls to write out a list of stereotypes they believe to be true, as well as ones that have been used against them in the past. By acknowledging and moving past stereotypes, we can challenge the notions of girlhood and womanhood that so often hold us back. It starts with us.

5. Avoid being critical of others or calling them out to drag them down. Most of us are guilty of having made judgements about people based on a small amount of knowledge or observation of their lives. It's not only unkind to make judgements, but also deeply unfair.

Gaslighting – something girl power is not

The term 'gaslighting' originated from the 1938 play *Gas Light*. In the film, a woman's husband slowly manipulates her into doubting her own mind. The term has been used colloquially since the 1960s to describe efforts to manipulate someone else's perception.[113]

The aim of gaslighting is to make someone think they are paranoid, overreacting or oversensitive. It ensures that this person can't engage in a genuine disagreement. Gaslighting might not be intentional, and may be a defence mechanism, but it does lead to worrying impacts on those experiencing it.

Gaslighting is often observed in unhealthy friendships.[114] It's not uncommon for girls who are controlling to find ways to shift blame, lie or twist or reframe conversations in a way that makes those on the receiving end become extremely anxious or even experience breakdowns. When girls are dealing with people who never acknowledge their thoughts, feelings or beliefs, they'll begin to question themselves.

The gaslighter gains power by trivialising others' emotions.

Here's what gaslighting might sound like among young girls:

- 'You're crazy.'
- 'Don't be so sensitive.'
- 'I was just joking.'
- 'Don't get so worked up.'
- 'You're totally imagining things.'
- 'It doesn't mean anything.'

Adopting an attitude of gratitude

Most of us feel gratitude regularly. Getting a good grade, scoring a tricky shot in a game or even making it to the bus on time are all things that may spark gratitude briefly. This fleeting feeling may elicit happiness and satisfaction in the moment, but it likely won't lead to lasting change.

Scientists have begun to research and examine what happens to individuals who practise gratitude regularly, and the results are pretty incredible. Gratitude has been shown to lead to overall improvements in our happiness, life satisfaction and connections with others, changing mindsets.[115] The earlier we can start this practice, the better off we'll be. If our daughters adopt a regular practice of gratitude as teenagers, the positive effects in their lives can be far-reaching.

Many academic and scientific studies over the last several years have tried to pinpoint just how gratitude affects our overall mindset. Research has shown that teenagers and adults who feel grateful more often than others are also happier, get better grades and have better friendships. They also sleep better, have more energy, and fewer illnesses and less pain.[116] Another study found that gratitude can improve relationships in both personal and work settings.[117]

One study of 300 adults, mostly college students, found that those who wrote letters expressing their thanks for something another person did experienced better overall mental health than those who either wrote about negative experiences or didn't write anything at all.[118] By helping us focus on positive emotions, practising gratitude primes our brain to be more sensitive, making it easier to recognise and acknowledge positive emotions we experience in the future.

One of the easiest ways to train your brain to focus on gratitude is to keep a gratitude journal. This is something simple your girl can do. All she needs is a notebook, or even a dedicated file on her computer. Either daily or weekly, she can jot down a few notes of gratitude. It needn't be a significant or time-consuming task – in fact, it's better to write short notes frequently, whenever these thoughts come to mind.

Another way to better embrace gratitude is to reframe the way in which we say 'thank you'. Many of us say this so often that it becomes rote. We should encourage our girls to be more specific about their gratitude. Here are some examples of what they can say instead of a casual 'thanks' when someone has performed a favour or an act of kindness:

- 'Hey, I appreciate you doing X for me.'

- 'I'm grateful for your kindness.'

- 'When you took the time to do X, it meant a lot to me. Thank you.'

Key points to land on

Adopting the habit of spreading kindness is a magnificent game changer, especially if this habit is solidified during the teenage years. Kindness is a characteristic that will serve girls throughout adulthood, and hopefully they'll model it for others.

To help your teen be kind to herself, encourage her to notice when she's doing these things and to do everything possible to banish them from her day-to-day routine:

- Ignoring her inner voice
- Beating herself up for things she can't fix
- Forgetting to rest
- Trying to please everyone at the risk of hurting herself
- Comparing herself with others
- Ignoring her dreams

Acts of kindness don't need to be grand or time-consuming. Here are some examples of things girls can do to spread kindness:

- Buy a movie ticket for the person behind them
- Pay for someone's meal at a restaurant
- Write letters to elderly relatives
- Donate Christmas gifts to the homeless
- Participate in a fundraiser
- Use their allowance to donate to a charity
- Hold the door open for someone
- Thank a teacher with a note, drawing or homemade gift

SEVEN
Unleashing Your Power

Before taking off

'You are your best thing.'[119] This quote from Toni Morrison is such a powerful reminder for our girls to accept and embrace themselves as they are. The power that girls need to be their best selves is already within them.

This is the truth, but who goes about teaching them how to harness and unleash it? What in our curricula actively ensures that our girls believe this? They need to be taught to unlearn what they've picked up through osmosis. They need to know that they're likely chasing some ideal that isn't real or attainable, and they need to appreciate how far they can go if they're supported in the right way.

We often worry so much about where we wish to see our girls go that we forget to look back at where their journey started. Striving for growth is instrumental in shaping our girls, but the value of appreciating and celebrating progress along the way is what makes it all worthwhile. This chapter explores a more personal journey of mine to illustrate what epitomises elevating our girls for a better future.

P is for power

You can create *power* from the challenges you face. Our goal as parents and educators is to ensure young girls subscribe to this belief: 'There is only one me. It's my journey, and in it, I can be my own superhero.' Mapping out ways to transform challenges into super-powers is an exciting part of the journey. Let's nurture girls who are lifted by their uniqueness and recognise that it's what makes them truly special.

My personal journey underpins the KWP framework of understanding yourself, celebrating your strengths and nurturing your wonders and worries in order to unleash your power. The framework can help shape our lives at pivotal stages of our development and growth. In sharing my story in the pages that follow, I hope to enable more people to embrace themselves and their individuality. It's my aspiration to see girls learning to live harmoniously in a society made up of all the differences which together create the most beauty in the world.

One of my first toys was a doctor's kit. I have several photographs of me dressed up as a doctor and performing check-ups on my siblings. Whether this cultivated my love for science or if I had it innately and my parents were intuitive enough to see it, I'm not sure. Regardless, this set me on a trajectory to pursue the sciences and one day become a physician. By the time I was in high school, my goal was to become a paediatric oncologist. I spent many summers volunteering at camps for kids who were undergoing cancer treatments and watched them with admiration for their strength. I wanted to cure their illnesses so that they could confidently say, 'When I grow up, I will...' secure in the belief that they had a future ahead of them. Cancer was something I was determined to beat and gain revenge on for selfishly taking my mother away from me.

Despite my best efforts throughout high school and university, I didn't make the cut. I failed the Medical College Admission Test (MCAT) miserably. I could blame my part-time jobs for the lack of time to study enough, or the nerves I had on the day, but in truth, I'm not entirely sure why I failed to turn up. Whatever the reasons, the rude awakening felt like a hard punch to my stomach. I'd spent my teen years and university life gearing up for this event. I'd convinced myself that surely my hardships as a young teen were meant to lead me to medical school so that I could become the best doctor ever known – the doctor who cured cancer so that no one would ever experience the pain I had. I was devastated, and I had no plan B.

After much grieving, I resigned myself to thinking that I'd just have to apply again the following year. Pursuing any other career options or courses wasn't a route I was prepared to consider. I'd study harder and more seriously than before for the MCAT. I also decided this was my opportunity to spend more time with my maternal grandparents, who were in India. I hadn't seen them since I was a little girl, and the urge to travel through India to learn more about my roots while also reconnecting with my grandparents appealed to me. So off I went. The events that followed were life changing. The discovery of new places, the unveiling of the deeper parts of my roots and the quality time with my grandparents and relatives were more fulfilling and enlightening than I could have imagined.

I perfected speaking, reading and writing in Hindi and uncovered some of my grandma's best-kept-secret curry recipes. I listened intently to my grandfather's tales about his days in the police force and about how he prided himself on his daughters. It was, without my realising it at the time, the best form of therapy for me.

During this visit, one of my uncles in North India invited me to accompany him to an orphanage that he was involved in running. The welcome by the children was electrifying. I read stories in English with some of them, and they were enamoured by the most minute gestures of love shown to them. This experience completely altered my view on what I wanted to do with my life. Could it have been that the career I was so desperate to pursue wasn't my purpose after all? Was teaching and working with children in fact my calling?

I never did reapply to medical school. Back home in Canada, I applied for a programme that would earn me an education degree and subsequently graduated from the middle years teaching programme with honours. My time in India was the most enlightening year. The pressures I'd been putting on myself dissolved and I realised I wasn't letting myself down by not trying again to become a doctor. I replaced guilt with reflection and spent time listening to the quieter, subtle messages that spoke my truth. My inner voice led me to discover the fact that teaching was my *superpower*. I've genuinely loved each and every day of being a teacher. I've gained inconceivable delight in the opportunities that have come my way and the extraordinary connections that I've made with colleagues and students and their families.

In the midst of completing my degree, I was recruited for a teaching job in London. It was in the last six months of this two-year teaching contract that I met the incredible man I married. Becoming a mother and learning about our son's diagnosis enabled me to expand my strategies for connecting with and teaching pupils whose brains were wired in different ways. It was raising a vulnerable young girl of my own that ignited my passion to draw on all my Ks and all my Ws in the hopes of creating space for Ps to shape the way young girls view themselves.

Through each of my 'failures', I've learned that the easy option is to blame oneself and play the victim. Examining each hardship presented and facing it with the tools that I've shared in this book can enable us to accept that all our challenges occur for reasons often greater than us. They exist to fuel a sense of purpose and shine light on the higher truths of life that are out there waiting for us to reach for and embrace – to pursue an experience, a journey or an education that is richer and more meaningful and that will truly elevate our existence if we let it. If we look deeper into ourselves and take time to comprehend who we are inside, our light will penetrate through and shine brightly on the outside in due course.

This will propel us towards raising girls who dare to dream.

Staying empowered and influencing others

Teen girls are only beginning their incredible journeys. The tools they gain, the skills they learn and the stories that inspire them will keep them moving forward. Challenges will come, but as we've discussed, expecting *and* accepting hardship is one of the greatest ways to overcome it.

Once their unique superpowers are unleashed, our girls will be able to transform themselves and rise from these difficult times in an informed and positive way. They will have a new outlook and stronger armour, and no one can ever take these things from them. They will be able to continually add layers of power to sustain their strength and beliefs.

For our girls to honestly accept themselves, they must learn to understand the gifts of imperfection, the value in their individuality, the beauty in their differences. If they can use their own force for positive change, they'll likely inspire other girls to accept themselves too.

Personal growth

It's fundamental to remember that personal growth isn't a linear process. Bad days are going to be part of growing up, so we need to provide our girls with encouragement, to let them know that even if one day is particularly hard, there will be brighter moments to come. Occasionally, these bad days will include making mistakes in judgement. That's what makes us human. We must teach our girls to embrace the act of learning from mistakes and untangling themselves from any shame or guilt associated with making errors.

It's also vital that our girls understand the difference between personal growth and constantly comparing themselves to others or wishing for something else. With expectations of themselves that are too high, our girls won't be living the life they have in front of them, which will indeed lead to utter dissatisfaction. Goals and dreams for the life they aspire to should be balanced with mindful acceptance of the present – of the good and the bad, of themselves wholly.

Being authentic

'Authenticity' is currently a buzzword. At this stage of development, girls are still working out so much about who they are and what they hope to be. It's important to help girls grapple with the enormous pressure that comes with projecting one idyllic image of themselves – the 'authentic' version. It's unrealistic for them to present a static version of themselves in every situation, and unhealthy for them to think that they should. Instead, I encourage girls to identify with who they feel they are in terms of values and subscribe to the notion that there are different sides to each of us – a compilation or series of authentic selves.

It's essential for young girls to understand that each side of their identity is something that can evolve as values and beliefs change.

Our girls will find huge freedom in the fact that they don't have to present themselves to the world as anything other than who they are, and that they don't have to present every side of themselves to everybody they interact with.

Final thoughts on perfectionism

Girls need to know that they are loved and celebrated for the perfectly perfect imperfections that make each of them who they are. We must help them accept that no version of perfection exists and encourage them to surround themselves with people who will cherish them because of their imperfections, not in spite of them. It can be tough to learn that life doesn't always go to plan and that it doesn't look like how Instagram might be presenting it. Once girls develop self-belief and acceptance and love for the person they are and will continue to become, however, they'll know that they can see themselves through whatever life presents to them, even the most trying and testing challenges. They will have the power to embrace their own hero's journey.

Remember, breaking the ideas around perfectionism begins with us adults, who need to be introspective also. Here's another personal example.

The burden I carried to be the 'perfect' mother was the one I found myself cracking under. Perhaps it was because my mother wasn't around in my teen years. I dreamt of being the best mother to my kids, as I felt my own mother was with her children. I made a pact that I'd emulate everything she did and would deliver on the standards I set myself. I had big shoes to fill – I knew that.

Along the way, I added many benchmarks. I made myself believe that to be the best mother possible, I had to be on parent committees and at every school pick-up and drop-off, exercise enough to look fit at the school gates, bake cakes that looked like art for the bake sales, cook everything from scratch, grow the vegetables and herbs I used to cook their organic meals, maintain a career and a tidy home, host only the most creative play dates and, of course, never get cross! Well, no surprises here, I didn't attain this 'perfect' version of motherhood.

I worked tirelessly to recreate the pages of the White Company catalogue, where angelic children play peacefully in their pristine clothes as their mother sips coffee and admires her work with pride. The one thing I didn't account for was how messy life can get. No matter how hard you try, not everything can stay white and neat and orderly. What's more, colours, even those darker, messier ones, are what make life worth living. I needed to embrace the full range of the rainbow while remembering to savour the precious moments of calm and peace when they occurred. I was setting the most unrealistic standards and continually raising the bar each time I achieved a win only to stretch myself further. This wasn't sustainable.

I hope our girls will recognise this cycle much sooner than I did. I hope that they'll be brave in seeking help and courageous in speaking up and setting appropriate boundaries in their lives. Their paths will look brighter if they deem themselves important enough to nurture and invest energy in. This is the groundwork that will remind them that they are perfect just the way they are.

There's no trophy at the end of this strange thing called life. It's not everything we achieve materially but how we make people feel that will make the greatest impact and leave lasting impressions in the world. It's not a medal, nor GPA averages. It's the way my mama made me feel so important. I hold on to this over everything else.

Let's encourage our girls to go out there and be the ultimate superheroes by enlightening others through example. I hope you'll be able to use what you've gained from these five steps to not only unleash your own daughter's power, but also empower others along the way. I've learned through my own journey that anything that was meant for you won't miss you. Don't be afraid to try new things, seize new opportunities and encourage others along the way to do the same.

Key points to land on

We're all on a lifelong journey of learning and unlearning. There is so much potential within each of our girls, and we can help equip them for the task of unlocking it. I hope that whenever their minds throw resistance at them, or that whenever their vulnerability gets the better of them, they'll push through, owning, loving and knowing their worth. It's my wish for them to show up for others, but most importantly for themselves.

It's my wish to see them elevated.

The journey isn't straightforward. The road will be bumpy, and accepting this will provide a greater sense of achievement and ownership in regards to the outcomes. The utter joy of seeing our girls flourish, spread their wings and fly will surely be worth every effort. They will inevitably surprise and delight us with all they're empowered to do. Their freedom to be who they are will, I hope, also liberate the adults around them. Remember that we can learn from those who are younger, more junior or perhaps less experienced but equally if not more enlightened when it comes to paving the way for a purposeful existence of passion and curiosity.

Conclusion

I wrote this book with a vision of exploring how we begin empowering the young girls of today so they rise to limitless achievements and fulfil their desires and hopes – free from self-doubt. It's critical for girls to be led by a sense of curiosity and discovery, for them to think like seekers, scientists and explorers.

My aim is to teach girls what strong women are – those who build each other up through the superpowers of empathy and kindness instead of tearing each other down. I wish to equip girls with the resilience they need to get back up from the falls they may take and to demonstrate the courage necessary to accept and share vulnerabilities.

I hope that this book has illustrated the immense value of love – of loving oneself in order to spread that same love to others. Once girls love who they are, they hold the power to be whatever they want. As put so brilliantly by Melinda Gates, 'a woman with a voice is, by definition, a strong woman'.[120] But the search to find that voice can be remarkably difficult. Through support, mentorship and guidance, we must instil in our girls the confidence to search for their voice and make their thoughts heard. This is what will enable us as a society to move forward and flourish with compassion, ambition and bravery. Like anything learned, bravery needs to be practised, modelled and taught – so let us celebrate girls by doing just that, and in the process, also express gratitude to all the women who have come before us to pave the way, and to those who will continue to represent us in the future.

Two years ago, I left the formal classroom. It was a daunting prospect. I was nervous about leaving my happy and safe place – an organised classroom in one of the best schools of London. As I explain to the girls I work with, though, if opportunity knocks and we don't answer the door, we may never know what there is to find. Moving abroad and working on a new venture enabled so much of my personal journey to unfold. I created a programme to focus on what I believe are the greatest foundations for young girls. I was initially taken over by worries in my mind, but my heart whispered encouragement, and that's the voice I decided to invest in. After all, we can only regret the things we don't try. This is what formed the genesis of my passion project to lift and empower girls, so that they too would have the courage to listen to their own hearts. With renewed conviction and drive, I began to deliver on a promise that I'd made to myself about living each day for both my late mother and me. Working with and mentoring girls using the five steps described in this book has been one of my greatest joys. More emphasis needs to be placed on helping girls see beyond perceived boundaries and on issues such as mental health, as witnessed in the recent Tokyo Olympics with role models such as Simone Biles and Naomi Osaka.[121]

As a mother of a fourteen-year-old girl, I don't wish to convey that I have all the answers to parenting or teaching teens. What I have distilled within these pages and the mentorship programme is my experience working through the loss of my role model in my teen years, spending hours on playground duty in various schools (where often the greatest nuggets of knowledge about students are discovered), holding countless meetings and sessions with parents and school staff regarding the challenges on each side, and working out the complexities of a neurodiverse brain in raising my son. The chapters of my journey accumulated into the lessons that I've shared in this book. While I cannot offer all the answers, I can urge you to create safe spaces for young girls, where they're not judged. Elevate.RA aims to act as a neutral force between girls and their peers, family and even schoolwork. Together, my goal is to enable girls to create a new positive relationship with their minds, understand and appreciate the bodies they've been given, and build on their unique and wonderful personalities and identities, while thinking about the young adults they're working towards becoming. Evolving and becoming *you* is a lifelong process.

Each girl's journey will lead her onto roads that curve and bend sharply, have bumps of all sizes and even contain some dead ends. The key is to persevere, to keep taking the next step. Sometimes those steps will steer her backwards for a period, but this is also part of moving forwards.

We can help young girls map some of their journeys out and encourage them to embrace the excitement of the unknown so that they aren't apprehensive about taking on the future and can ride the road ahead with full security, knowing that they can always reach for their newly acquired tools. We can enable girls to feel empowered to put on their capes and soar.

'Here's to strong women. May we know them. May we be them. May we raise them.'[122]

Here's to girls who want to dream *big* and achieve *bigger*.

Notes

1 CJ Van Lissa et al., 'Common and unique associations of adolescents' affective and cognitive empathy development with conflict behavior towards parents', *Journal of Adolescence*, 47 (2016), 60–70, https://doi.org/10.1016/j.adolescence.2015.12.005; M Guasp Coll et al., 'Emotional intelligence, empathy, self-esteem, and life satisfaction in Spanish adolescents: Regression vs. QCA models', *Frontiers in Psychology*, 11 (2020), https://doi.org/10.3389/fpsyg.2020.01629

2 'Facts and figures: Economic empowerment', UN Women (July 2018), www.unwomen.org/en/what-we-do/economic-empowerment/facts-and-figures, accessed 24 September 2021; 'Girls' education', UNICEF (19 January 2020),

www.unicef.org/education/girls-education;
'Girls' education', Theirworld (23 August 2021),
https://theirworld.org/explainers/girls-
education

3   M Arain et al., 'Maturation of the adolescent
brain', *Neuropsychiatric Disease and Treatment*, 9
(2013), 449–461, https://doi.org/10.2147/NDT.
S39776

4   L Sax, 'How social media may harm boys and
girls differently', *Psychology Today* (12 May 2020),
www.psychologytoday.com/ca/blog/sax-
sex/202005/how-social-media-may-harm-boys-
and-girls-differently, accessed 24 September
2021

5   CJ Van Lissa et al., 'Common and unique
associations of adolescents' affective and
cognitive empathy development with conflict
behavior towards parents', *Journal of Adolescence*,
47 (2016), 60–70, https://doi.org/10.1016/j.
adolescence.2015.12.005; M Guasp Coll et al.,
'Emotional intelligence, empathy, self-esteem,
and life satisfaction in Spanish adolescents:
Regression vs. QCA models', *Frontiers in
Psychology*, 11 (2020), https://doi.org/10.3389/
fpsyg.2020.01629

6   D Campbell, 'Stress and social media fuel
mental health crisis among girls', *The Guardian*
(23 September 2017), www.theguardian.com/
society/2017/sep/23/stress-anxiety-fuel-
mental-health-crisis-girls-young-women,
accessed 1 October 2021

7 R Anand, 'Author and Academic Katherine Rundell', *The Elevate Podcast* (29 December 2020), www.elevate-ra.com/podcast, accessed 1 October 2021

8 'The problems of over-scheduled teens', Middle Earth (28 August 2017), https://middleearthnj. org/2017/08/28/the-problems-of-over-scheduled-teens, accessed 1 November 2021

9 I Amed et al., 'The influence of "woke" consumers on fashion', *Our Insights*, McKinsey (12 February 2019), www.mckinsey.com/industries/retail/our-insights/the-influence-of-woke-consumers-on-fashion, accessed November 2021

10 A Khan, 'Happiness may bring you more money, study says', *Los Angeles Times* (19 November 2012)

11 M Gawdat, *Solve for Happy: Engineer your path to joy* (North Star Way, 2017)

12 'Kamala Harris: The vice president', WH.GOV (12 April 2021), www.whitehouse.gov/administration/vice-president-harris, accessed 1 October 2021

13 SR Cruess et al., 'Role modelling: Making the most of a powerful teaching strategy', *BMJ*, 336 (2008), 718–721, https://doi.org/10.1136/bmj.39503.757847.BE

14 R Anand, 'What's keeping girls out of STEM?', Elevate.RA (28 January 2021), www.elevate-ra.com/thoughts/whats-keeping-girls-out-of-stem, accessed 1 October 2021

15 'Brain development', First Things First (16 September 2019), www.firstthingsfirst.org/ early-childhood-matters/brain-development, accessed 1 October 2021

16 'Physical changes in puberty', Raising Children Network (13 July 2021), raisingchildren.net. au/pre-teens/development/puberty-sexual-development/physical-changes-in-puberty, accessed 1 October 2021

17 'Carol Dweck: A summary of growth and fixed mindsets', Farnam Street blog (March 2015), fs.blog/2015/03/carol-dweck-mindset, accessed 1 October 2021

18 SL Smith et al., 'Gender bias without borders', USC Annenberg, annenberg.usc.edu/sites/ default/files/MDSCI_Gender_Bias_Without_ Borders_Executive_Summary.pdf, accessed 1 October 2021

19 'Understanding the teen brain', University of Rochester Medical Center Health Encyclopedia, reviewed by J Campellone and RK Turley (no date), www.urmc.rochester.edu/encyclopedia/ content.aspx?ContentTypeID=1&Content ID=3051, accessed 1 October 2021

20 M Gawdat, *Solve for Happy: Engineer your path to joy* (North Star Way, 2017)

21 R Anand, 'Serial Entrepreneur and Author Mo Gawdat', *The Elevate Podcast* (9 February 2021), www.elevate-ra.com/podcast, accessed 4 October 2021

22 'Neuroplasticity', Arrowsmith Program
(5 February 2020), arrowsmithschool.org/
neuroplastic, accessed 1 October 2021

23 B Arrowsmith-Young, 'The woman who
changed her brain', author website, https://
barbaraarrowsmithyoung.com/woman-who-
changed-her-brain, accessed 1 October 2021

24 RY Erol and U Orth, 'Self-esteem development
from age 14 to 30 years: A longitudinal study',
Journal of Personality and Social Psychology, 101/3
(2011), 607–619, doi:10.1037/a0024299

25 M-R Abraham, 'Dark is beautiful: The battle to
end the world's obsession with lighter skin', *The
Guardian* (4 September 2017), www.theguardian.
com/inequality/2017/sep/04/dark-is-
beautiful-battle-to-end-worlds-obsession-with-
lighter-skin, accessed 1 October 2021

26 A Ossola, 'The media's effect on women's body
image', News & Events, Hamilton College (1
September 2010), www.hamilton.edu/news/
story/the-medias-effect-on-womens-body-
image, accessed 1 October 2021

27 'Girls on beauty: New Dove research finds low
beauty confidence driving 8 in 10 girls to opt out
of future opportunities', Dove (5 October 2017),
www.prnewswire.com/news-releases/girls-on-
beauty-new-dove-research-finds-low-beauty-
confidence-driving-8-in-10-girls-to-opt-out-of-
future-opportunities-649549253.html, accessed 1
October 2021

28 'Behind the selfie: Reversing the damage of digital distortion', Unilever (21 April 2021), www.unilever.com/news/news-and-features/Feature-article/2021/behind-the-selfie-reversing-the-damage-of-digital-distortion.html, accessed 1 October 2021

29 'Our mission,' Dove US, www.dove.com/us/en/dove-self-esteem-project/our-mission.html, accessed 1 October 2021

30 'Mentors: Image & self esteem', Council on Alcoholism and Drug Abuse, cadasb.org/mentors-image-self-esteem, accessed 1 October 2021

31 S Savage, 'New national report reveals the high price of low self-esteem', RedOrbit (7 October 2008), www.redorbit.com/news/health/1580382/new_national_report_reveals_the_high_price_of_low_selfesteem, accessed 1 October 2021

32 T Weinstock, 'Breakout Gucci beauty star Ellie Goldstein says it's time for more models with disabilities', *Vogue* (7 July 2020), www.vogue.co.uk/beauty/article/ellie-goldstein-interview, accessed 1 October 2021

33 Ibid.

34 'Eating disorders in teens', American Academy of Child and Adolescent Psychiatry (March 2018), www.aacap.org/AACAP/Families_and_Youth/Facts_for_Families/FFF-Guide/Teenagers-With-Eating-Disorders-002.aspx, accessed 1 October 2021

35 'ARFID statistics & facts', Eating Recovery
    Center, www.eatingrecoverycenter.com/
    conditions/arfid/facts-statistics, accessed 1
    October 2021

36 H Yahghoubi and A Mohammadzadeh,
    'Comparison of perfectionism and related
    positive-negative dimension in people with
    high traits on obsessive compulsive and eating
    disorder characteristics', *Iranian Journal of
    Psychiatry and Behavioral Sciences*, 9/3 (2015),
    https://doi.org/10.17795/ijpbs-264

37 I Dudova et al., 'Suicidal behavior and self-harm
    in girls with eating disorders', *Neuropsychiatric
    Disease and Treatment*, 12 (2016), 787, doi:10.2147/
    ndt.s103015

38 'Eating disorders', *Mayo Clinic*, Mayo Foundation
    for Medical Education and Research (22 February
    2018), www.mayoclinic.org/diseases-conditions/
    eating-disorders/symptoms-causes/syc-
    20353603, accessed 1 October 2021

39 T Wiseman, 'A concept analysis of empathy',
    Journal of Advanced Nursing, 23/6 (1996), 1162–
    1167, doi:10.1046/j.1365-2648.1996.12213.x

40 A Grant, *Think Again: The power of knowing what
    you don't know* (WH Allen, 2021)

41 G Itzchakov et al., 'The listener sets the tone:
    High-quality listening increases attitude
    clarity and behavior-intention consequences',
    Personality and Social Psychology Bulletin, 44/5
    (2018), 762–778, doi:10.1177/0146167217747874

42 KG Kugler and PT Coleman, 'Get complicated: The effects of complexity on conversations over potentially intractable moral conflicts', *Negotiation and Conflict Management Research*, 13/3 (2020), 211–230, doi:10.1111/ncmr.12192

43 'Types of listening', *Fundamentals of Public Speaking*, Lumen Candela, https://courses.lumenlearning.com/atd-fscj-publicspeaking/chapter/types-of-listening, accessed 1 October 2021

44 'Auditory processing disorder', Nemours Foundation, reviewed by TL Riegner and D Inverso (February 2021), kidshealth.org/en/parents/central-auditory.html, accessed 1 October 2021

45 S Sinek, 'Hearing is listening to what is said. Listening is hearing what isn't said', *LinkedIn* (2020), www.linkedin.com/posts/simonsinek_hearing-is-listening-to-what-is-said-listening-activity-6741924509055504384-Adta, accessed 1 October 2021

46 B Brown, 'Listening to shame' TED Talk, TED (16 March 2012), www.youtube.com/watch?v=psN1DORYYV0, accessed 30 October 2021

47 B Brown, *Daring Greatly: How the courage to be vulnerable transforms the way we live, love, parent, and lead* (Penguin Life, 2015)

48 B Brown, 'Daring classrooms', author website (August 2019), www.brenebrown.com/daringclassrooms, accessed 30 October 2021

49 S Gordon, 'How teaching kids empathy can prevent bullying', *Verywell Family*, Dotdash

(1 July 2021), www.verywellfamily.com/teach-empathy-and-prevent-bullying-460744, accessed 30 October 2021

50 J Probert, 'Leading with empathy in the pandemic', Saïd Business School (1 July 2020), www.sbs.ox.ac.uk/oxford-answers/leading-empathy-pandemic, accessed 1 October 2021

51 L Cerniglia et al., 'Intersections and divergences between empathizing and mentalizing: Development, recent advancements by neuroimaging and the future of animal modeling', *Frontiers in Behavioral Neuroscience*, 13 (2019), https://doi.org/10.3389/fnbeh.2019.00212

52 'Bullying statistics', Family Resources Furtherance Project, www.frfp.ca/bullying-statistics, accessed 1 October 2021

53 Rutgers University, 'Teen girls more vulnerable to bullying than boys', *ScienceDaily* (7 May 2019), www.sciencedaily.com/releases/2019/05/190507110457.htm, accessed 1 October 2021

54 M Waseem and AB Nickerson, 'Bullying', *StatPearls* (July 2021), www.ncbi.nlm.nih.gov/books/NBK441930, accessed 1 October 2021

55 'Upstander', Facing History and Ourselves, www.facinghistory.org/upstander, accessed 1 October 2021

56 M Waseem and AB Nickerson, 'Bullying', *StatPearls* (July 2021), www.ncbi.nlm.nih.gov/books/NBK441930, accessed 1 October 2021

57 'How can we help kids with self-regulation?',
    Child Mind Institute, www.childmind.org/
    article/can-help-kids-self-regulation, accessed 1
    October 2021

58 J Segal et al., 'Improving emotional intelligence
    (EQ)', HelpGuide (12 October 2021), www.
    helpguide.org/articles/mental-health/
    emotional-intelligence-eq.htm, accessed 30
    October 2021

59 A Ovans, 'How emotional intelligence became a
    key leadership skill', *Harvard Business Review* (28
    April 2015), hbr.org/2015/04/how-emotional-
    intelligence-became-a-key-leadership-skill#,
    accessed 1 October 2021

60 C Raypole, 'Big feels and how to talk about
    them', *Healthline*, Healthline Media (10
    September 2019), www.healthline.com/health/
    list-of-emotions, accessed 30 October 2021

61 C Raypole, 'How to handle interpersonal conflict
    like a pro', *Healthline*, Healthline Media (11
    February 2020), www.healthline.com/health/
    interpersonal-conflict, accessed 30 October 2021

62 C Raypole, '12 signs of low emotional intelligence
    — plus tips for building it', *Healthline*, Healthline
    Media (24 February 2021), www.healthline.
    com/health/mental-health/low-emotional-
    intelligence, accessed 30 October 2021

63 D Goleman, 'What makes a leader?', *Harvard
    Business Review* (January 2004), https://store.
    hbr.org/product/what-makes-a-leader/
    r0401h?sku=R0401H-PDF-ENG, accessed 30
    October 2021

64 K Stringer, 'What's an emotion scientist? Inside the new concept shaping social-emotional learning', The 74 (5 August 2019), www.the74million.org/whats-an-emotion-scientist-inside-the-new-concept-shaping-social-emotional-learning, accessed 1 October 2021

65 A Ovans, 'How emotional intelligence became a key leadership skill', *Harvard Business Review* (5 May 2015), https://hbr.org/2015/04/how-emotional-intelligence-became-a-key-leadership-skill, accessed 30 October 2021

66 NH Bailen et al., 'Understanding emotion in adolescents: A review of emotional frequency, intensity, instability, and clarity', *Emotion Review*, 11/1 (2019), 63–73, doi:10.1177/1754073918768878

67 A Purcell and W Zuckerman, 'Brain's synaptic pruning continues into your 20s', *NewScientist* (7 August 2011), www.newscientist.com/article/dn20803-brains-synaptic-pruning-continues-into-your-20s, accessed 1 October 2021

68 WA Brechwald and MJ Prinstein, 'Beyond homophily: A decade of advances in understanding peer influence processes', *Journal of Research on Adolescence*, 21/1 (2011), 166–179, doi:10.1111/j.1532-7795.2010.00721.x

69 N Tottenham and A Galván, 'Stress and the adolescent brain: Amygdala-prefrontal cortex circuitry and ventral striatum as developmental targets', *Neuroscience & Biobehavioral Reviews*, 70 (2016), 217–227, doi:10.1016/j.neubiorev.2016.07.030

70 NH Bailen et al., 'Understanding emotion in adolescents: A review of emotional frequency, intensity, instability, and clarity', *Emotion Review*, 11/1 (2019), 63–73, doi:10.1177/1754073918768878

71 S Avishai-Eliner et al., 'Developmental profile of messenger RNA for the corticotropin-releasing hormone receptor in the rat limbic system', *Developmental Brain Research*, 91/2 (1996), 159–163, doi:10.1016/0165-3806(95)00158-1

72 'Bullying prevention in schools', Public Safety Canada (31 January 2018), www.publicsafety. gc.ca/cnt/rsrcs/pblctns/bllng-prvntn-schls/ index-en.aspx#a01, accessed 30 October 2021; M Brackett and S Rivers, 'Preventing bullying with emotional intelligence', *The Conversation* (18 October 2021), https://theconversation. com/preventing-bullying-with-emotional- intelligence-25992, accessed 30 October 2021

73 C Rim, 'Brené Brown and Marc Brackett on emotional intelligence during a pandemic', *Forbes* (24 April 2020), www.forbes.com/sites/ christopherrim/2020/04/24/bren-brown-and- marc-brackett-on-emotional-intelligence-during- a-pandemic/?sh=b3a86bbc0ae2, accessed 30 October 2021

74 'Homepage', RULER Approach/Yale University (2021), www.rulerapproach.org, accessed 30 October 2021

75 Yale Center for Emotional Intelligence, www. ycei.org, accessed 1 October 2021

76 Podcast, Dr Marc Brackett and Brené Brown
    on 'Permission to feel' (14 April 2020), https://
    brenebrown.com/podcast/dr-marc-brackett-
    and-brene-on-permission-to-feel

77 A Grant (@AdamMGrant), 'A core skill of
    emotional intelligence is treating your feelings as a
    rough draft...' (6 September 2020), https://twitter.
    com/adammgrant/status/1302618190019727360,
    accessed 1 October 2021

78 C Rim, 'Brené Brown and Marc Brackett on
    emotional intelligence during a pandemic',
    Forbes (24 April 2020), www.forbes.com/sites/
    christopherrim/2020/04/24/bren-brown-and-
    marc-brackett-on-emotional-intelligence-during-
    a-pandemic/?sh=b3a86bbc0ae2, accessed 30
    October 2021

79 G Hopkins, 'Journal writing every day: Teachers
    say it really works!', Education World (2010),
    www.educationworld.com/a_curr/curr144.
    shtml, accessed 1 October 2021

80 Day One, dayoneapp.com

81 B Khoury et al., 'Mindfulness-based therapy:
    A comprehensive meta-analysis', *Clinical
    Psychology Review*, 33/6 (2013), 763–771, https://
    doi.org/10.1016/j.cpr.2013.05.005

82 DM Davis and JA Hayes, 'CE Corner', *American
    Psychological Association*, 43/7 (2012), www.apa.
    org/monitor/2012/07-08/ce-corner, accessed 1
    October 2021

83 A Grant (@AdamMGrant), 'A mark of emotional
    intelligence: treating unpleasant feelings not

as unwelcome intrusions but as teachable moments. Regret is a seminar on making wiser choices. Guilt is a class on doing the right thing. Boredom is a course on finding flow. Anxiety is a tutorial on preparation.' (6 October 2020), https://twitter.com/adammgrant/status/131 3466765146546177?lang=en, accessed 1 October 2021

84 K Stringer, 'Social-emotional learning boosts students' scores, graduation rates, even earnings, new study finds', The 74 (12 July 2017), www.the74million.org/article/social-emotional-learning-boosts-students-scores-graduation-rates-even-earnings-new-study-finds, accessed 1 October 2021

85 H Keller, *The Story of My Life* (Doubleday, Page & Co, 1903)

86 M Ungar, *I Still Love You: Nine things troubled kids need from their parents* (Dundurn, 2014)

87 SR Bird and JA Hawley, 'Update on the effects of physical activity on insulin sensitivity in humans', *BMJ Open Sport & Exercise Medicine*, 2/1 (2017), https://doi.org/10.1136/bmjsem-2016-000143

88 'Exercise can boost your memory and thinking skills', Harvard Medical School, *Harvard Health Publishing* (15 February 2021), www.health.harvard.edu/mind-and-mood/exercise-can-boost-your-memory-and-thinking-skills, accessed 1 October 2021

89 'Exercise', The Centre for Personal Performance,
    personalperformance.com.au/exercise-boosts-
    performance-resilience, accessed 1 October 2021

90 MS Khan et al., 'Low serum brain-derived
    neurotrophic factor is associated with suicidal
    ideation in major depressive disorder',
    Psychiatry Research, 273 (2019), 108–113, https://
    doi.org/10.1016/j.psychres.2019.01.013

91 R Richter, 'Among teens, sleep deprivation
    an epidemic', *News Center*, Stanford Medicine
    (8 October 2015), https://med.stanford.edu/
    news/all-news/2015/10/among-teens-sleep-
    deprivation-an-epidemic.html, accessed 1
    October 2021

92 E Suni, 'How much sleep do we really need?',
    Sleep Foundation (10 March 2021), www.
    sleepfoundation.org/how-sleep-works/how-
    much-sleep-do-we-really-need, accessed 1
    October 2021

93 E Suni, 'Mental health and sleep', Sleep
    Foundation (18 September 2020), www.
    sleepfoundation.org/mental-health, accessed 1
    October 2021

94 'Melatonin: What you need to know', *National
    Center for Complementary and Integrative Health*,
    U.S. Department of Health and Human Services,
    www.nccih.nih.gov/health/melatonin-what-
    you-need-to-know, accessed 1 October 2021

95 'School start times for adolescents',
    PEDIATRICS, 134/3 (2014), 642–649, https://
    doi.org/10.1542/peds.2014-1697

96 TS Sathyanarayana Rao et al., 'Understanding nutrition, depression and mental illnesses', *Indian Journal of Psychiatry*, 50/2 (2008) 77, https://journals.lww.com/indianjpsychiatry/toc/2008/50020

97 R Anand, 'Author and Academic Katherine Rundell', *The Elevate Podcast* (29 December 2020), www.elevate-ra.com/podcast, accessed 1 October 2021

98 KJ Gough, 'Why perfectionism in girls is so pervasive – and how to change it', Detroit and Ann Arbor Metro Parent (11 September 2020), www.metroparent.com/parenting/tweens-teens/why-perfectionism-in-girls-is-so-pervasive-and-how-to-change-it, accessed 3 October 2021

99 'APA Dictionary of Psychology', *American Psychological Association*, https://dictionary.apa.org/learned-helplessness, accessed 1 October 2021

100 R Simmons, 'Why failure hits girls so hard', *Time* (25 August 2015), https://time.com/4008357/girls-failure-practice, accessed 1 October 2021

101 C Dweck, 'What having a "growth mindset" actually means', *Harvard Business Review* (13 September 2021), https://hbr.org/2016/01/what-having-a-growth-mindset-actually-means, accessed 1 October 2021

102 J Shamsian, 'How J.K. Rowling went from struggling single mom to the world's most successful author', *Insider* (31 July 2018), www.

insider.com/jk-rowling-harry-potter-author-biography-2017-7, accessed 1 October 2021

103 J Samuel, *This Too Shall Pass: Stories of change, crisis and hopeful beginnings* (Penguin Life, 2020)

104 Ibid.

105 University of California, Berkeley, 'Social scientists build case for "survival of the kindest"', *ScienceDaily* (9 December 2009)

106 'Forget survival of the fittest: It is kindness that counts', *Scientific American* (26 February 2009), www.scientificamerican.com/article/kindness-emotions-psychology, accessed 3 October 2021

107 D Keltner, 'The compassionate species', The Greater Good Science Center (31 July 2012), greatergood.berkeley.edu/article/item/the_compassionate_species, accessed 3 October 2021

108 J Holt-Lunstad et al., 'Social relationships and mortality risk: A meta-analytic review', *PLoS Medicine*, 7/7 (27 July 2010), https://doi.org/10.1371/journal.pmed.1000316

109 N Tate, 'Loneliness rivals obesity, smoking as health risk', WebMD (4 May 2018), www.webmd.com/balance/news/20180504/loneliness-rivals-obesity-smoking-as-health-risk, accessed 3 October 2021

110 M Greenberg, 'About', author website (25 January 2021), https://drmelaniegreenberg.com/about, accessed 1 October 2021; J Breur, 'Homepage', Dr Julia Breur LLC, www.drjuliabreur.com, accessed 1 October 2021

111 A Bethea, 'An open letter to corporate America, philanthropy, academia, etc.: What now?', Medium (1 June 2020), https://aikobethea. medium.com/an-open-letter-to-corporate-america-philanthropy-academia-etc-what-now-8b2d3a310f22, accessed 3 October 2021

112 R Anand, 'Mother, Transgender Activist, and Pediatrician Paria Hassouri', *The Elevate Podcast* (22 March 2021), www.elevate-ra.com/podcast, accessed 3 October 2021

113 K Abramson, 'Turning up the lights on gaslighting', *Philosophical Perspectives*, 28/1 (2014), 1–30, doi:10.1111/phpe.12046

114 'What it's like to be gaslit by a friend', *Cosmopolitan* (13 April 2021), www. cosmopolitan.com/uk/love-sex/relationships/ a31777005/gaslighting-friends, accessed 1 October 2021

115 'Giving thanks can make you happier', Harvard Medical School, *Harvard Health Publishing* (14 August 2021), www.health.harvard.edu/ healthbeat/giving-thanks-can-make-you-happier, accessed 1 October 2021

116 A Alkozei et al., 'Gratitude and subjective wellbeing: A proposal of two causal frameworks', *Journal of Happiness Studies*, 19/5 (2018), 1519–1542, https://doi.org/10.1007/ s10902-017-9870-1

117 DE Forster et al., 'Benefit valuation predicts gratitude', *Evolution and Human Behavior*,

38/1 (2016), 18–26, https://doi.org/10.1016/j.
evolhumbehav.2016.06.003; JJ Froh et al.,
'Counting blessings in early adolescents: An
experimental study of gratitude and subjective
well-being', *Journal of School Psychology*, 46/2
(2008), 213–233, https://doi.org/10.1016/j.
jsp.2007.03.005

118 J Brown and J Wong, 'How gratitude changes
you and your brain', The Greater Good Science
Center (6 June 2017), greatergood.berkeley.edu/
article/item/how_gratitude_changes_you_and_
your_brain, accessed 4 October 2021

119 T Morrison, *Beloved* (Alfred A Knopf, 1987)

120 MF Gates, 'Remarks from 2003 Powerful
Voices Luncheon', GatesFoundation.org, www.
gatesfoundation.org/Ideas/Speeches/2003/10/
Melinda-French-Gates-2003-Powerful-Voices-
Luncheon, accessed 1 October 2021

121 'Olympics: Support for Simone Biles, Naomi
Osaka shows progress on mental health', *The
Straits Times* (8 August 2021), www.straitstimes.
com/sport/olympics-support-for-simone-biles-
naomi-osaka-shows-progress-on-mental-health,
accessed 1 October 2021

122 Original source unknown; 'Lily Collins gets
letter from Michelle Obama', AP NEWS (18
April 2017), https://apnews.com/article/
michelle-obama-lily-collins-a552bccbf66d4cfeb7
a4fe07ffcf3194, accessed 1 October 2021

Further Reading

Arrowsmith-Young, Barbara, and Norman Doidge, *The Woman Who Changed Her Brain* (HarperCollins Publishers, 2020)

Bajpai, Amita, and Meenakshi Dwivedi, *Learning Disability: Uncover the myths* (Kalpaz Publications, 2017)

Biddulph, Steve, *10 Things Girls Need Most: To grow up strong and free* (HarperThorsons, 2018)

Biddulph, Steve, *Raising Girls in the 21st Century: From babyhood to womanhood – helping your daughter to grow up wise, warm and strong* (Simon & Schuster Australia, 2019)

Damour, Lisa, *Untangled: Guiding teenage girls through the seven transitions into adulthood* (Atlantic Books, 2017)

Doidge, Norman, *The Brain That Changes Itself: Stories of personal triumph from the frontiers of brain science* (Penguin Life, 2017)

Eide, Brock L, and Fernette F Eide, *The Dyslexic Advantage: Unlocking the hidden potential of the dyslexic brain* (Plume, 2012)

Forgan, James W, and Mary Anne Richey, *Raising Girls with ADHD: Secrets for parenting healthy, happy daughters* (Routledge, 2014)

Grossberg, Blythe N, *Asperger's Teens: Understanding high school for students on the autism spectrum* (Magination Press, 2015)

Icard, Michelle, *Fourteen Talks by Age Fourteen: The essential conversations you need to have with your kids before they start high school* (Harmony, 2021)

Jain, Renee, and Shefali Tsabary, *Super Powered: Transform anxiety into courage, confidence, and resilience* (Random House Books for Young Readers, 2020)

Nadeau, Kathleen G., et al., *Understanding Girls with Attention Deficit Hyperactivity Disorder* (Advantage Books, 1999)

Quinn, Patricia O, *Attention, Girls!: A guide to learn all about your AD/HD* (Magination Press, 2009)

Samuel, Julia, homepage, www.juliasamuel.co.uk

Siegel, Daniel J, *Brainstorm: The power and purpose of the teenage brain* (TarcherPerigee, 2015)

Siegel, Daniel J, and Tina Payne Bryson, *The Whole-Brain Child: 12 revolutionary strategies to nurture your child's developing mind* (Bantam, 2012)

Syed, Matthew, *Bounce: The myth of talent and the power of practice* (Fourth Estate, 2010)

Toeps, Bianca, *But You Don't Look Autistic at All*, translated by Fay MacCorquodale-Smith (Toeps Media, 2020)

Walker, Beth, *The Girls' Guide to AD/HD: Don't lose this book!* (Woodbine House, 2004)

For girls to read

Kay, Katty, et al., *The Confidence Code for Girls: Taking risks, messing up, & becoming your amazingly imperfect, totally powerful self* (HarperCollins Publishers and Blackstone Audio, 2018)

Khaira, Raj Kaur, *Stories for South Asian Supergirls* (Kashi House, 2019)

Rebel Girls, *Rebel Girls of Black History: A sticker-by-number book* (Dial Books, 2021)

Thompson, CaShawn, et al., *Good Night Stories for Rebel Girls: 100 real-life tales of Black girl magic*, edited by Lilly Workneh (Rebel Girls, 2021)

Acknowledgements

This book couldn't have been written without the endless patience and incredible support from my family. Rigorous days of homeschooling and working-from-home challenges along with the countless other ups and downs the global pandemic presented left us all a bit worn thin. My family's flexibility and encouragement granted me opportunities and motivation to write even on days I didn't want to, renewing my sense of self. They believed in me before I did.

To each and every one of my students – from the day I first set foot in a class as a student teacher to the day I started taking my own classes as a newly qualified teacher and the day I became a department head, you have taught me and given me a gift greater than I could ever have imagined. I think of you and applaud your inquisitive minds and curious questioning, your emotional outbursts, and your incredible wit and intelligence regularly. Thank you for letting me in. To the parents who have entrusted their daughters to me since the launch of Elevate.RA, your getting behind me and taking on my vision so wholeheartedly was the catalyst for getting this book out. I admire and thank you very much.

To every guest who so kindly and bravely shared their journey on my podcast series, your voices and messages provide me with hope for our girls and have reinforced the pressing need to empower our girls so that they continue to smash those glass ceilings.

To the best mentor I could have asked for as a growing teacher, Sally Ashcroft; the ever-inspiring and encouraging Katherine Rundell; the eternal optimist, best supporter and life coach, Andrew Sheridan; and for his honesty and reassurance, Robin Walden. Thank you all for taking such care of my thoughts and treating my words with the utmost love and encouragement.

Thank you to my editor, Kate Latham, and the team at Rethink Press and Jordana Weiss for getting behind this project and helping me achieve a goal I didn't think I was capable of, particularly in this, well, most unpredictable year.

The Author

Ramita Anand is the founder of Elevate.RA, an educational mentoring service designed to empower young girls to help them lead remarkable lives. She has more than fifteen years of experience working with students in classrooms and in one-on-one settings. She's a Canadian-trained teacher who has worked and taught in Vancouver, London, New York and Singapore and the mother of a teen girl and a pre-teen boy. Her experiences in education and parenting have given her a unique platform, from which she has designed methods and programmes to empower young girls.

To learn more, check out The Elevate Podcast (available on all podcast platforms or on www.elevate-ra. com/podcast) or get in touch on her website or on social media.

🌐 www.elevate-ra.com

❑ facebook.com/elevatera.edu

❑ www.linkedin.com/in/ramitaanand

◎ @elevate.ra

To learn more about how the Elevate.RA mentoring programme and other services can support you and/ or your daughters or schools, please do get in touch at info@elevate-ra.com for a free consultation.

Made in the USA
Monee, IL
28 February 2022

92026995R10115